Down The Cayman Wall
The True Story Of The Largest Shark Ever Seen

By
Gary Montemayor

Ilustrations created by Photoshop

*For
Laura*

PREFACE

Man with his ingenious imagination has managed to walk on the moon, land probes on mars and build a modern world whose knowledge is growing exponentially. Humanities boundaries seem limitless even stretching to the periphery of the seemingly impenetrable. However, man also has an imagination that creates ghost, goblins and giant hairy men walking in the forest and unsubstantiated dragons peaking their head up in waters frequented by visitors. Thus when one talks of unusual sightings that don't conform to the traditional encounters with creatures, it is met with skepticism.

Sea monsters in particular are shrouded in myth. Legend has it that these aberrations of creation, deformed and perverted by the deep's hellish pressure, have from time to time revealed themselves to those who dared journey from the shore. The heavens may be on earth but hell was in the sea.

Over time however the myth has turned to reality and the number of sightings of sea monsters has dwindled. Even as more eyes enter the deep sea, one would think that there would be more discovery, more stories that would fill the hearts and minds of future explorers, but this is not the case. Current statistical studies on sea monsters done by Dr. Charles Paxton of St. Andrews University in Scotland show a small number of large creatures yet to be discovered. This is in sharp contrast to the teachings of a bountiful ocean filled with giants and weird glowing animals tumbling through a black enigmatic sea. Yet it is my experience that in just a one mile stretch of deep ocean and literally thousands of submersible dives at this site I have encountered phenomena of powerful forces that have attacked our submersible, a prehistoric gigantic species of shark, a glowing light seemingly without matter and a simultaneous coincidental smell of smoke in the sub, evidence of a sea monsters lair and glimpses of large fish-like tails that didn't resemble anything we have encountered before. Moreover, move just one more mile from this realm and a new book can be written, like a new hood filed with fresh stories of precocious new phenomena.

Even though statistically we are not encountering giant glowing beast in the deep like I had imagined when I first dove into the deep, it is my determination that there are other even more seemingly inauspicious enigmas cloaked in the eternal black of the deep cold sea.

Each dive I have lead I have been accompanied by other observers that have experienced right along with me these curiosities and have interpreted them with similar conclusions.

These sightings must be documented because of the increasing number of eyes that are probing the depths and their stories must be compared.

1

"I'm lost." The soft-spoken confession from the man sitting next to me brought me back from my thoughts. I could tell that my co-pilot had turned his head to look at me, but in the near blackness of 500 feet below the surface I could barely make out his silhouette, let alone his expression. His voice however, was heavy with concern. It was easy to get disoriented in the deep, especially when someone was new to the job. Jason was the first trainee I'd ever worked with who lacked essential seamanship skills. When I first met him he even had trouble tying a bowline knot.

"Do you know where we are?" he asked."God, I hope so, or we're both in big trouble," I replied, smiling.

Jason laughed and turned on a red light in the dark cabin to check our depth gauge. I didn't need instruments to tell me where we were. The shadowy undersea landscape outside the view port was as familiar to me as my own mind. Its visual beauty was a map I had committed to memory a long time ago.

"Looks like we're at about 570 feet and falling," I said, surmising our position from the near absence of light and the distant appearance of the first "haystacks." The stacks were portions of the Cayman Wall that had eroded into pointed limestone towers. We were inside the Mesopelagic zone, a place that modern explorers called "The Twilight Zone." Jason was a pilot trainee assigned to me for instruction in deep sea navigation and we were huddled together in the front belly of a small, yellow research submersible, breathing humid air and falling in slow motion and total darkness down an undersea mountain cliff. Our objective was a place as deep as the Empire State Building was tall, 1200 feet below the surface. Such tremendous depth may be skyscraper size on land, but in the 23,600-foot Caribbean trench called the Bartlett Deep, it was only a dimple. The huge jaws of this underwater Grand Canyon yawned beneath us.

"Man, Gary, you called it dead-on," said Jason with a laugh. "We're at 575 right now." He turned his red lamp to low and shook his head. "I don't know how you can be so damn sure of where you are in this dark. I always gotta check the instruments."

"Well, that's a good thing," I said immediately, building his confidence. "Just because you get familiar with the area you are diving in doesn't mean you can slack off on safety in any way, especially when you're approaching these stacks. It can be awfully easy to run into one of them. I still double check my instruments."

Deep-sea manned submersibles were an endangered species for good reason. In this age of computer-operated remotes, it's not only less expensive to send down an unmanned Remotely Operated Vehicle with a camera to get information; it's also a hell of a lot less dangerous. An ROV is a robot, tethered by an umbilical that instantaneously sends pictures and data to an operator who is relaxing with a cool beverage onboard a safe, air-conditioned, surface ship. Remotely Operated Vehicles (ROV's) could stay down far longer than their human counterparts ever could because ultimately, human beings will always be slaves to their hunger for oxygen. Still, there was a good reason why I was training down this far with Jason, and the look on his face as he peered out into the ocean in front of us said it all. My co-pilot was transfixed; eyes open wide in a strange mixture of delight and terror. The hairs that stood up on the back of his neck had captured him, heart and soul, in a way that no soullessly acquired video feed ever could. Jason was a mild-mannered guy, twenty-seven years old with a face that still had some traces of innocence on it, especially when he was at the controls of this sub. Although I was a few years his senior, I felt a little paternal towards him. I knew exactly what he was feeling and I smiled.

"Don't worry" I assured him. "In time, you'll get to know the area as well as I do."

I twisted open a water bottle and tried to find a comfortable place to put my feet in the tiny cabin. The area we were sharing was only about 48 inches in diameter inside the big fish-eye view port in the front of the sub, the floor was bumpy with exposed stainless steel pipes and circuit breaker boxes that controlled the machinery. It had been an extremely hot day on the surface, so it seemed unusually stuffy since our descent, and it all served to make me feel a little cramped. Thankfully, we were falling at 65 feet a minute and I knew that at 600 feet, the sub would finally begin to cool, as it always does. Condensation would bead up on the walls inside and drip on us. The first cool drop was a welcome relief and I wiped it off my already damp forehead. Finally at ease, I started thinking how Jacques Cousteau had once said that to explore under the sea is to know what it means to "move like an angel," and I rolled my shoulders to relax them, imagining that the sub was my own personal set of wings.

"Approaching 1000 feet," Jason called out.

"Okay," I said, "I'll take it from here." Jason passed the six-inch control box to me and I placed it between my thighs, curling my legs up, yogi-style, in front of the 32 inch bubble view port of the sub, a hemisphere made of 2.5 inch thick bullet-proof acrylic Lexan. The ocean produced a pressure of about 530 pounds per square inch at 1200 feet, enough to crush a large Styrofoam cup into the size of a rigid thimble, just an inch or two tall. A car tire carried about 40 PSI by comparison, and a straining champagne cork shot out of a bottle at about 90 PSI. Here, an entire ocean was pressing against our view ports and it would only get heavier as we went deeper. At 1500 feet, the stubby Perry Class sub we were riding in would literally collapse on itself from the pressure, so Jason and I needed all the protection we could get. Crush depth was just one of the reasons a pilot must watch his instruments so carefully. A few feet could literally be the difference between life and death.

I turned on the outside lights briefly to check our rate of descent by watching the particles pass by the port. When I snapped them off again, a scarlet flicker against the darkness below us caught Jason's eye.

"Hey, look at that," he said pointing.

A glistening, luminescent Ctenophore made an entrance, materializing out of the darkness into our view port. The incandescent like lights of the small animal, no more than the size of a fist, were on full wattage as it fluttered towards the sub, forcing us to take notice of his arrival. Ctenophores are pelagic animals, bulbous in shape, and they swim by beating bands of small cilia, which lay in two vertical rows on their sides, like a thousand tiny arms. Because these bands looked very much like the teeth on a comb, Ctenophores have earned the nickname "Comb Jelly." This particular Comb Jelly's bioluminescence, a glow in the dark quality shared by many deep-water species, was singularly beautiful. Each cilium around his glossy, transparent body reflected a resplendent red and was quivering in perfect synchronicity, making him appear as if he was made of pure, blinking neon. We paused to watch him.

"I think he might have been attracted to our lights," reasoned Jason, "because he sure is strutting his stuff. Maybe he thinks were a big, beautiful she-jelly." he grinned.

"I doubt it," I said and laughed. "Comb Jellies are hermaphroditic."

We watched the animal's flashy display for a moment more before Jason asked quietly, "Do you think that if I walked into the Lone Star Bar tonight, all lit up like a freakin' crystal chandelier the way that thing is, that some girl would notice me?"

Jason had a Northwest "dude" quality to him. He was deeply tanned, and forever clad in flip-flops and baggy shorts. When he wasn't learning to pilot the sub, I understood that he worked as golf pro in Vancouver.

"I don't know," I said shrugging. "I guess that depends on whether or not you want to hook up with a woman who gets turned on by hermaphrodite jellyfish. Judging by the way Biff gets dates though, some women seem to be."

"Good point." Jason snorted, and then turned his gaze towards the surface. "God, imagine how cool it would be though if you could actually light up like that. Especially if you could pick the parts of you that you wanted to light up."

"Yeah, well, I'll tell you what, Jason" I said with a serious tone, but smiling. "You can hang all the lights you want on a stinkweed, but that ain't gonna make it no Christmas tree."

Jason turned to me in surprise, saw that I was smiling, and laughed.

The Ctenophore wasn't alone for long. A strange-looking Salp, about six inches long, woozily tumbled end over end off the port side of the window, interested in what was going on here. A Salp was a transparent, living tube, with a shapeless, unsegmented body that secretes a mucus-like film. This viscous adhesive ran along their entire body and Salp used it to collect microbial food from the sea as well as to cling to others of their kind in colonial chains that could reach up to 60 feet long. Some of these long, swimming Salp orgies have been mistaken for sea monsters in days gone by, but this particular Salp was going it solo, and its slow motion ballet was mesmerizing.

It was a different planet at this depth. Creatures like Salps and Comb Jellies might look odd to us surface types, but in truth, we were the quaint looking aliens down here. The Cayman sub-sea terrain was otherworldly; a vast abyssal scrape that falls several thousand feet downward at a 45-degree angle. The area we were descending in was covered with particulates that had fallen for all eternity from the sunny photosynthetic Epipelagic zone of shallower water above, a dusting of blue-gray "sea snow" that gave the landscape a lonesome Death Valley look. The occasional, jagged, limestone haystack that projected upward only accentuated its austerity. I always half expected to see a sun bleached cow skull lying somewhere around this deep island slope. The haystack zone looked and acted as a fortress, separating the sparse deep where we were, from the colorful, vibrant, calypso world of Cayman sponge belt nearer the surface. As divers dropped down the wall, the gorgeous tropical seas of the first few hundred feet changed all at once to the cold, blue-black abyss, and the transformation made a pilot feel slightly off balance. As if he had just stepped from a lush garden to the inside a cold murky tomb. Smart explorers knew however, that no matter how dark and lifeless the abyss might seem, the ocean below 1000 feet was actually teeming with life. Hundreds of creatures were attached to each of the limestone stacks, like brittle stars, sea whips and stalked crinoids. And then there were the creatures you didn't see, animals like the Coffinfish, the rare Six Gill shark, and maybe even a Giant Squid.

I had Giant Squid in particular on my mind that day because I had just finished reading all about them the night before in Richard Ellis' book, The Search for the Giant Squid. The language of that book stuck with me like a lingering dream, coloring my perception of the waking world and making me peer even harder into the darkness, just in case something terrible was lurking out there. According to Ellis, Giant Squid specimens of up to 65 feet in length, twenty feet longer than a bus, and weighing more than a ton have already been found, and that's unlikely to be the largest of them. Arthur C. Clarke is quoted in that book as saying, 'it would be strange indeed if the world's biggest squid had been among (those) very few cast ashore." It may very well be that there are thousands of unseen Giant Squids growing to 150 feet or more.

Perhaps the strangest fact about Architeuthis (Gary, it would be best to have this pronunciation guide as a footnote at the bottom of the page, what do you think? (Ark-uh-TOO-this)), as the Giant Squid was scientifically known, however, was that no one had ever actually seen a living, breathing example of one anywhere on earth. It's only from the occasionally beached corpse that we were certain they exist, and although that settles the usually debated question about sea monsters, which was, "are they real?" the greater mystery of Architeuthis was how a creature so large has managed to escape the almost certain detection of modern sonar and other recognition technologies for so long. It was believed that Giant Squid lived everywhere, from Greenland to New Zealand, and yet, they all remained unseen, the sea's own masters of disguise. The usual specimen of Architeuthis washed up mysteriously on beaches in giant stinking tangles of enormous tentacles, often hideously decomposed. A few of the best carcasses would still have the squid's complex 10 inch eyeballs intact, and some remains have even been found slowly digesting in the guts of captured Sperm Whales. But that was all we really knew about them. The Sperm Whale snack specimens offered our only clue about where Architeuthis fell on the food chain, and even then, it was only a hint. Sperm Whales with large sucker marks, presumably from doing battle with Giant Squid and losing, have also been found dead, washed up along the shoreline. Dissections of Giant Squid corpses hadn't shed much light on the mystery surrounding these animals, either. All that autopsies had ever revealed was that they were great big animals with very empty bellies, so there was simply no telling where a Giant Squid hid himself and what he might eat. I did know for a fact that at least one smaller squid, the 10-foot Humboldt, could be a nasty tempered fellow who ate its own kind and attacked humans. It made my imagination wonder if an "invisible" Giant Squid might be hungrily watching our exposed sub from inside a haystack.

I sure hoped so. I longed to be the first person to capture a living Architeuthis on film, and I would have given my good hat and both boots if today could be the day. I reached down and patted the camera that was waiting at my side.

Inside, it was time to check the life support gauges. Jason and I were breathing recycled air and we depended on a bit of mechanical ingenuity called "the scrubber" to clean the cabin of toxic CO_2 gases and artificially add the proper amount of oxygen. All levels looked normal and we were fully prepared to put down for a while. I turned on the sub's outside lights, and the solitary white beam reflected back billions of particles of swirling sea snow, sharply altering my vision. I could just make out the outline of a haystack among the particulates. It was a giant boulder with a flat shelf in front, perfect for landing the sub. Perfect also perhaps, as a hiding place for that Squid.

"Well touch down there," I said to Jason. "Stand by for a jolt."

I carefully positioned the sub above the chosen spot and released the upthrusting vertical, lowering us a bit a time until, at last, the sub's skids dug into the murky seafloor, stirring up a silty blur that enveloped us. The sudden cloud took its precious time settling down and I used the opportunity to set up my gear so I would be able to film whatever happened by the view port. I carefully mounted the camera on the crossbar directly in front of the big window, and looking through the lens. I saw the haze from the sediment finally parting like a stage curtain. Behind it, a shape emerged, becoming clearer and clearer, until it finally revealed itself to be a beautiful glass sponge. White and delicate, like a small, frozen explosion of ice hanging off the limestone haystack and glittering in our spotlight.

"Wow," said Jason, twisting his head to take it all in, "That sure is a pretty thing. I know it's not a moving animal like you wanted, but I think you ought to get a few shots of it anyway, don't you?"

I certainly did. For a long while, the camera's engaging motor and the quiet whisper of oxygen flow from life support was all we heard. When we were satisfied with the shots, I shut the camera off and waited silently, in the total darkness of 1200 feet, for some new subject to come our way. Across the path of the sub's headlight, a large shadow suddenly appeared on the sloped ground directly in front of us, and my heart immediately beat a little quicker.

"Hey," I said, sitting bolt upright. "There's something moving around out there. It looked big, too by the size of the shadow." I pointed in its direction. "Let's follow it."

Jason smiled. "Makes sense to me."

I put down the camera and picked up the video-game-like joystick that controlled the sub. We rose, and took a slow banking turn around a rock. There, we paused to search the area, but there didn't seem to be anything around us. Still, I could sense that there was something nearby; a presence that my instincts said was watching us. It's hard to explain the sixth sense that develops after time. It begins on the very first voyage. Right away, it's realized that the deep, the true deep, was a harsh and predatory place, frightening in exactly the same way that being alone in a dark forest was on the surface world. Forget what's been said about the delicate and beautiful fairyland of the sea. The Abyss was Darwinian survival in its basest sense. Over time a sub pilot learns to sense when the atmosphere around has changed. Squinting into the darkness, I could only make out one creature, and it certainly wasn't animal enough to make a shadow as big as the one Jason and I had just seen. It wasn't the presence I was feeling. It was just another Salp, large and transparent, but it was a pretty darned interesting Salp nonetheless. Small wonder we hadn't seen it at first because, except for a bit of bioluminescence, this guy was nearly invisible.

I had developed the habit of assigning the creatures I run into down here a personality, though I'm never quite sure if the traits I give the animals I see come from their actions or just from the spark of imagination that happens inside me whenever I am lucky enough to run into one of them. It seemed to me that this little Salp was acting absolutely drunk on swallowed seawater. Moving in a whirling reverie, he was slowly and deliberately opening and closing his feeding tube, gulping down copepods. He was alone, about ten inches long, and with a six-inch tail that was thick with a spiral of copepods. The inside of him was lit up like tiny lightening bolts, and he was lost in his own pleasure, paying absolutely no attention to anything around him. Gulping relentlessly, he hit the view port, turned left, and just kept swallowing. It made me laugh to watch his unbreakable concentration.

"Are those things like jellyfish?" asked Jason. He had not yet had any training in Deep Sea Marine Biology. His major interest was in piloting the sub.

"Not exactly," I explained. "They look a lot like jellies, but they have a primitive notochord, like a backbone." I ran my finger along the view port to trace the barely visible outline of an undeveloped spine on the dancing animal. "See it? Some people think that pelagic Salp are the missing link between vertebrates and invertebrates. This one's really unusual, though." I said with admiration. "Look at the size of him."

Jason squinted at the creature. "Oh yeah," he said, "I see his spine! We should get him on film, too, you know. I like the way he moves."

He did have a certain rhythm to his gluttony. We filmed him for several minutes, marveling at the divine machinery that was a Salp. They all had hollow bodies that worked exactly like a jet engine, taking water in the front, and squirting it out the back to propel themselves along in slow-motion undulation.

"This is fantastic," I said, with one eye squinted shut and the other fixed on getting the moving critter in frame through the camera's viewfinder. Jason and I were both lost in the dance, hypnotized by the graceful image and concentrating so hard on keeping the moving Salp in frame that I forgot all about the eerie sensation of being watched. All my attention was riveted on the movement of the feeding. Open and shut. Open and shut. I started to breathe in rhythm with the movement.

"Times up, guys," interjected a shrill voice from the surface over the UWT. I nearly dropped the camera into my lap, startled back to consciousness. The nasal voice of surface support, oblivious to its imposition went on. "You need to surface now, Gentleman because I have a plane to Havana I really need to catch. Do you copy?"

I shot a glance at Jason, who was also trying to act as if he hadn't just had the shit scared out of him. He swallowed hard, skin pale, then picked up the handset to reply.

"Roger that," he said, with his voice creaking just a bit on the "oger." He cleared his throat and went on. "We're on our way back up."

I shut down the camera, nerves still tingling from my rude re-entry into consciousness, but, in spite of the adrenaline-fueled heart attack, I was pleased beyond words at the footage I had just taken. Jason seemed to read my mind.

"Good stuff you got today, Gary," he said.

"Thanks," I said, unscrewing the mounts. "Couldn't have done it without you, though."

We had gotten some first-class material. Getting decent underwater shots was only as hard as finding the animal's habitat, however finding the habitat in the deep is pure luck. The ocean was staggeringly huge, covering 71% of the world's surface with over 140 million square miles, at an average depth of 12,200 feet. And in all of that that area, it was estimated that there were only about 500,000 to 10 million marine species roaming around in it. In a best-case scenario, an undersea filmmaker was likely to encounter about fourteen animals every ten square miles. In the deep sea, the odds were even slimmer than that because most marine creatures live in clusters above 500 feet. With such disheartening statistics, just knowing where to look and having technical filmmaking skills was not enough to get the kind of footage needed to rock Jacques Cousteau's world. Having a plate piled high with luck helps. Happily, lady luck was with us that day. Jason and I beat the odds and got something just fantastic on film. Who knew how long it would be until I ran into something exciting again? Feeling both thrilled and restless,

I sighed as I pulled the camera from the mountings and put the equipment away.

Too bad we didn't run into whatever it was that was hanging around us earlier, I thought to myself. Now that was a presence. Much larger game than a greedy little Salp. It had seemed a dark and heavy force, as if a predator were stalking us. Perhaps a shark was circling nearby, trying to determine if the sub were edible. I would have loved to have gotten a Giant Six Gill Shark on film. The very ions in the air seemed to say that it was possible, but the hard facts took precedent over my instincts. The truth was, we had only seen one hungry, little pelagic tunicate down here, and it sounded like surface support guy really needed to get to Cuba. I had to let any notions of finding and filming monsters go for now. It was time to concentrate on getting the sub back up safely.

Jason and I began to go over the checklist for ascent that every pilot has emblazoned in his memory.

"What's the Voltage?" I asked.

"122v main and 22 v on 24 volts system."

"Switch 24 volt system to reserve," I said. "Check to be sure your trim valves are in the correct position. I don't want to hear the full force of the sea in those pipes down here."

"Check," Jason replied.

"What's our HP Air?" I wondered out loud.

"700 Main and 2400 reserve."

That wasn't enough in the main. "Switch to reserve air for

the initial ascent," I said. "We will never be able to push air into the soft ballast with only 700psi in the system." I smiled. "Hell, its almost 600 PSI out there already."

Jason did as I asked.

"Okay," I said, "Trim switch on?"

"You got it," he said.

The pumps began coughing to life, and, with a roar that sounded like a lawn mower; water stared heaving out of the ballast tanks, pushing against the tremendous pressure gradient outside. I always marveled that this funny looking underwater mini-van's electric motors could manage to spit out enough water to move us along against the raging ocean currents so dutifully, but it always did, flying me exactly where I needed to go.

"Good Girl," I muttered under my breath. The praise made the electric motors show-off a little and the sub lifted smoothly into the darkness. As we began to ascend, I handed Jason the control box and crawled up into the tower, a round space just big enough for a single head and shoulders at the top of the sub. The tower is the true nerve center of the sub and the place where I usually sat when taking paying passengers down for an extreme adventure dive. I shined a light on the instrument panel and made a mental note that we were taking off at 1200 feet. The depth on this sub was being measured by a Bourdon tube assembly that was activated by a pressure bladder on the outside of the sub. A Bourdon tube may sound like some hard-core, high tech apparatus, but it works exactly like one of those polka-dotted, coiled party noisemakers that straighten out and honk when you blow into it. The pressure of the water makes the bladder straighten out, and the needle records the depth. In fact, many of the systems on the Perry Class research subs I operated ran on principles of physics that were about as sophisticated as the machinery on a golf cart. It worked well though. Simple pneumatic and hydraulic tools are often the best choice underwater, and they certainly got the job done. Our PC subs have two of these Bourdon pressure systems, one on each side, so the pilot could depend on redundancy for back up in case one side fails.

My heart lifted right along with the sub, and I started thinking about getting a burger and beer when we finally got back to the Island. I watched the depth gauge tick me a little closer to my "Cheeseburger in Paradise."

1180, it said . . . then 1170 . . . 1160 . . .

At 1150, a rocket hit us dead on. At least, it felt like a rocket. There was a tremendous boom. Smashing into us from below with a deafening sound. Catching my balance on the sides of the hull, I instinctively looked at the depth gauge. We were no longer rising. The sub had come to a complete halt. My neck burned a little, and we were still rocking in the water from the impact. All around us were darkness and silence.

"What in the hell was that?" I asked Jason. "What did we hit?"

Jason's voice had a panicky little laugh as he looked at the instruments. "Near as I can tell, nothing. I think something hit us." He immediately flicked on the outside lights, and the view was still. There was nothing to see but eternal, black emptiness. No haystacks, no critters, not even a silt cloud was stirring. The sub was running but we were bobbing in place, nose slightly downward.

"Check the systems, "I said to myself as much as Jason. "Are we okay, Damnit?"

Jason and I examined every detail of the instrumentation and cabin of that sub in less than twenty seconds flat. Probably a record somewhere.

"Why is our nose off-balance like that? Has the hull been breached?" Jason asked nervously. It was a good question. In fact, it was the only question. These PCs had life support for seven days. As long as the pod we were floating in was intact, we could survive and figure a way to surface.

"Negative," I said. "Believe me, Jason, you'd know if we'd been breached. The outside lights are working, and that means we still have power. That's all we need to get the hell out of here, so I suggest we do it." All at once, I felt very tired. "We've just had a fender bender with something," I said, trying to reassure him.

Jason looked around the deep-blue vacuum that surrounded us, then shrugged weakly. "With what?" he asked.

"Beats the hell out of me," I said, "but whatever it was, it was a big 'un, and I don't want to wait for it to come back. Let's go!"

Our oxygen and Co2 levels looked good, and all systems seemed normal. Then, the harassment on the UWT started again.

"1205, are you headed in or what? I gotta get out of here soon."

I pressed the switch and replied. "Roger, Surface, we are coming up. We've hit something down here though, so we'll need you to stand by."

"Copy that," the surface said, suddenly serious. "Damage report?"

I craned my head around the 360-degree view from the tower and cast my eyes down to look at as much hull as I could see. "Nothing to report so far, "I said, "but whatever hit us sure made me cometo Jesus."

"Are you moving?"

I hit the air ballast, and we began to rise.

"On our way up," I said, "but we'll need to be lifted so we can look the sub over for damage."

"We'll be waiting," was the reply.

After death, damage to the sub would be the next worst-case scenario. An out of commission submarine would mean that I, and God knows how many other people, would be out of work for a good long while; not a pleasant state of affairs on an isolated Island like Grand Cayman. For some, it would mean waiting tables for months on end at a tourist hotel. The vessel seemed okay, but I wouldn't know for certain until we got it out into the sunlight and could get a decent look at the outside. Every little cough of the motors echoed more than usual in the suffocatingly sultry cabin as I steadied the ship upwards. My only objective now was to get her back up in one piece.

I watched the needle on the depth gauge, and it offered progressively good news. When I felt certain we would make it, I let my mind wander back down into the deep for just a moment. I knew, in my very core, that the creature whose watchful presence I'd felt back there was the cause of this collision. Whatever it was that had been stalking the sub had been waiting for just the right moment to nail the hell out of it. The fact that the blow happened right after we started rising seemed to prove this theory. Any large marine animal would have seen the sub's charge upwards as a threat to its territory, and I was certain it was a moving object that hit us. It had to be. There was absolutely nothing stationary anywhere around for us to run into at that location. The landscape there was practically a void. I imagined that, somewhere in the distance below us, some Giant Squid was snorting with satisfaction at the way it showed that big, ugly yellow fish what to expect if it dares venture into its terrain again. Watching the yellow thing grow smaller as it scooted away, the sub would reflect in its huge, shiny eyeballs, and it would draw her mighty tentacles upwards in satisfaction, then rocket back to her hiding place for the undisturbed rest every victorious warrior deserves. With a quick whirl of silt, two enormous eyes would again disappear inside a black sea cave, watching from inside the lair for the next hapless intruder that had the cajones to cross its path. I looked down at my film equipment lying useless on the floor in the cabin and shook my head mournfully at the glorious footage I would not be getting. A chance like this would never come again.

The sub broke the ocean surface into rush of tropical air and the sudden brilliance of Caribbean sunshine streaming through the portholes in the tower made me squint in pain. Surface crewmembers scrambled onto the top of PC1205 and secured a chain to the giant metal hook that was just outside on the aft side. The sound of gears engaging could be heard in our cabin, and Jason and I felt the fluid clutch of the sea give way to the swinging loose sensation of being dangled in the air. An A-Frame hoist lifted the 8 and a half-ton submarine out of the sea and onto the deck of the mother ship. Once the vessel was secured, I immediately crawled out and started searching it, bow to stern, for any sign of damage.

"Hey, Gary!" called the maintenance supervisor Jacko, a fellow sub pilot as he walked towards us. "I hear you hit something down there!"

Jacko was just beginning his shift, and he had his arms crossed, head cocked back and a smile on his face, as if he had just accidentally run into me on the corner of Goring and Church Street. Jacko is consistently as pleasant as a Sunday afternoon no matter what is going on around him. Nothing fazes him, and everything fascinates him. He rocked back on his heels and twisted his head to the side to take in as much of the hull as he could with a single glance. "Doesn't look like there's anything noticeable on the skin though, and you guys sure made it up here in record time."

The usual ascent from that depth takes about twenty minutes. We had made it in fifteen. Another record.

"Sub parts must be working right," he concluded.

Jason's head appeared in the tower hatch, his face all pink and smiling. "You would have been in a rush, too," he said, putting his hands on either side of the hatch as he pushed himself up and out of the sub. "'Cause we didn't run into anything. We got hit."

Jacko drew his head back in surprise. "Got hit?" he asked. "By what?"

I sighed. "Well, that's what we'd like to know." I walked towards the prop, reaching my hand up and running it along the bottom of the black crashbar that ran the length of the sub. It occurred to me that perhaps the crashbar was all that would have saved us had there been a second attack.

"All I know, "I said, "is that whatever hit us was a solid as a rock. I mean, wham" I smashed my fist into my open palm. "It was like a meteor, except that it came from below. There was this loud metallic sound." I rubbed my neck. "And a jolt that I can still feel in my spine."

Jason nodded vigorously in agreement. "And when we looked for what was there, there was nothing around. I mean nothing. All we saw the whole trip was a Comb Jelly and a couple of Salp." He smiled. "Got some good pictures of them, though."

Jacko grinned at the student pilot. "So what do you think, Jason?" he asked. "After something like this you want to take the sub down to 1200 ever again?"

Jason may have been a little breathless, but he was more than sure of his answer. "Oh, God yeah, I'd do it again." He looked at me with a sly grin, then in a loud, whispered aside to Jacko, said, "But, you know. Maybe not with Gary. Still, though, I'd go back."

I smiled sarcastically and nodded my head. "Thanks for the vote of confidence, you little shit," I said. "Wasn't it you who was driving the sub?"

Jason laughed, and we continued the search for damage to the sub. After an hour of visual inventory and system checks, all seemed well and we decided to give up and make it official. The sub had sustained no damage. I walked across the steel grate deck of Igor, the mothership, pausing to pick up my gear bag and getting ready to board the launch that would take me to shore. Before I got onto chase boat, though, I looked back at the sub.

"Damnit, Jacko," I said to my friend who was standing beside me, "I know that something has to be wrong with that thing. You don't take a hit like that and just get off Scott free." I remembered how the sub's nose had listed downward just a bit after the crash. "Maybe I should have checked her stern a little closer." I said, taking a step towards the sub.

"Go home, Gary," said Jacko wisely, putting his hand on my shoulder and stopping me. "You can think everything to death, you know, and it won't help right now. Look, everybody's here, everybody's safe, and its time for you to go home and just relax for a while."

I could feel myself frowning, and conscious frowning is always a sign that its time to slow down. I puffed out my lips and made a deliberate attempt to relax my face.

"You're right. You're right," I said in resignation. "In fact I was thinking about a burger just before the crash, so I am outta here."

"Good boy," said Jacko, patting my shoulder, and I crawled into the launch and headed to shore.

Later that evening, showered and rested, I was walking along

Church Street, finally headed out to get that cheeseburger basket. It was twilight, and I was just in time to see the famous "Green Flash" of the Caymanian sunset. I paused to lean on a palm tree and wait for the show. The Green Flash was a natural green light that briefly lights up the horizon as the sun sets across the Caribbean. For it to happen however, the atmospheric conditions had to be just right, which they are about 50% of the time, but the flicker comes and goes so quickly, it could be hard to tell if it was a real glow or simply a trick of the eyes. Some clever photographers have managed great pictures of it over the years though, at least now and again. It really does exist. It's always a big question which nights it will appear. I smiled to myself in anticipation. Something as otherworldly as a green sunset could only happen here.

If one was lucky enough to be looking in exactly the right place, at exactly the right moment, there could be found a number of miracles waiting both above and below the stretch of ocean that I call "The George Town Rectangle." The Rectangle was a plot of water about a mile square off George Town Harbor that had become my own personal Bermuda Triangle because genuinely odd things seemed to happen out there. In the Rectangle that afternoon, I was hit by a mountain of an animal, and in that rectangle lay the ghostly remains of a ship named the Kirk Pride. One day in 1976, events, including rough weather, literally sucked the Kirk Pride from its docking space and out into the rectangle, where it sunk, exactly as if it were going down a drain. It was an ethereal piece of marine realty that would eventually come to dominate my life and my career, but at that moment, I just stood looking at the green flash above it in wonder, wishing I could capture the miracle in a jar to take home and study at my leisure.

When the sunset was over, I restlessly kicked a pebble and walked on explaining to myself that it is the nature of the miracles to remain unexplained. They always happened in a flash, here and gone before you could even blink, and a man could drive himself mad trying to figure out what they all meant. Still, for some unknown reason, humans are compelled to try and master everything. The frustration of it all was, I thought, why we invented burgers and beer.

I passed the squawking blue and gold macaw at the entrance to the Blue Parrot Bar and sat down on a rattan stool, more than ready to order. It was a weeknight, and the crowd was thin enough that I could make out a conversation or two among the folks around me as I waited for the bartender. A tourist couple behind me was quarreling over what to do with their last day on the Island. The woman wanted to go to Stingray City and swim with the rays, something you really can't do anywhere else on earth, but the husband was a little afraid of the animals. He didn't want to sound like they scared him, but both his wife and I could hear it in his voice. He was arguing in favor of the Turtle Farm he said, because the Sea Turtle is so endangered that seeing them and taking pictures could be something they could share with their Great Grandchildren. I thought that both of them made a good argument. Stingray City really is quite a sight. Years ago, fisherman cleaned their catches in that area, dumping the entrails into the sea and attracting hundreds of rays which in turn attracted hundreds of people standing in hoards on the nearby sandbar to see the rays. Today, the water in Stingray City was a beautiful blue, no more chum, because the rays were hand fed. It looked very inviting, and many folks waded in eagerly, thinking they were as safe there as a passenger on a theme park ride. In the end though, I had to give the debate to the husband on this one point alone: Funny thing about Stingrays is, they sting.

At long last, my beautiful burger arrived, grilled and plump, with just a bit of grease coating the soft bun, and I eagerly dove into it, savoring the salty taste of the meat and the crunch of the lettuce. I was so hungry, I bit in too deep, getting more than I could chew politely and my jaw muscles burned as I struggled to gnaw it all. I looked around surreptitiously, hoping no one would notice my stuffed mouth, and finally washed the huge gob down with a swig of beer. It was heaven. It was then I overheard two guys at the end of the bar talking about something that made the volume of all the other conversations around me drop to zero. They were talking about me.

"I dunno," said one of the men, a tall, tanned Canadian whom I recognized as one of the Dive Masters for Red Sail Sports at the Hyatt Regency. He took tourists on scuba expeditions. "All I heard was that something out there attacked the deep sub today."

His companion, a co-worker at Red Sail, looked exactly like his friend except that he had straight blond hair instead of curly. They were both dressed in red T-shirts and swim shorts. Neither one was wearing shoes. The second man nodded knowingly as if an attack like that was to be expected.

"Well, Jesus Christ," he said dangling an empty beer bottle from his thumb and forefinger and looking pleadingly at the bartender, "I don't doubt it. Who knows what the hell is swimming around down there? I think those guys who pilot those little subs are crazy going down that far. It's dark as sin and there are those prehistoric sharks down there, you know. Big ones."

"Yeah, I saw one time on TV where that "shark lady" that Dr. What's-her-name, got a sixteen footer on film," his friend shot back with a serious expression. "Imagine that? The shark you're filming is as long the sub you're sitting in. All that fish has to do is decide take one bite of one cable and you're a goner." He raised his beer to his lips, pausing to speak before he drank. "I'd rather stay up a little closer to the surface where I stand a chance of seeing daylight again thank you very much."

I wiped my mouth, grabbed my beer and got up to join them.

"Hey," I said, "I'm sorry. I didn't mean to eavesdrop, but I was listening to what you just said about the deep sub, and I know some guys who work over there. Where did you hear about it getting hit?"

"Oh," said the first one, pointing to his friend with the top of his curly head, "Elliot here's got a girlfriend that works at Soto's Dive Shop. Some guys were in there talking about it earlier today."

There was no faster method of communication then the coconut telegraph that was the gossip on Grand Cayman. I wanted to know more, though.

"Did she say if anything happened to the sub?"

"Well, I think they couldn't find anything wrong with it, but just between you and me, they couldn't pay me enough to go down on one of the goddamn yellow coffins after it had been in a collision like that."

I smiled. That was not an uncommon sentiment. Even without the collision, I couldn't tell you how many paying passengers had shelled out big money to go down on the sub, then bolted like jackrabbits just before I closed the hatch. The sub is no place for claustrophobic's that was for sure. I was curious why someone as clearly adventurous as two seasoned Divemasters wouldn't want to go down. "Why not?" I asked.

He looked at me as if I wasn't quite bright, and then spoke slowly so I could understand.

"Because if there is something wrong with that sub after they have given it a clean bill of health, they ain't gonna figure it out until they're too far down to do anything about it." He laughed. "Now maybe you wouldn't mind being stuck in pissed-up pants for a week in a tin can while you wait to be rescued, but I sure would."

I nodded in complete agreement, thanked them for the info, paid my bill, and went straight back to the launch. Hopping on first one foot, and then the other, I pulled off my topsiders and picked my way across the rocky shore to where the launch was tied, tossing the shoes in the boat. I immediately cast off, stepped over the side, and with a quick pull on the outboard, was on my way back out to the sub to see what I could have missed.

The night sky above Igor was as black as the ocean was deep, except for the pinhole lights of a billion stars. There was no light pollution in this part of the Caribbean so the starlight from this low hanging blanket was all I really needed to see by. To be certain I wasn't missing any details on the sub though, I turned on a few deck lights and trained them on the hull. It was strange how lifeless the sub looked sitting there in the amber lights. I had come to think of these subs as living breathing beings, but tonight, PC 1205 looked like a corpse on a slab in an autopsy. There had to be something on it somewhere that bore the scar of the day's collision. Something I hadn't thought of, but what? I pulled off my cap and ran my fingers through my hair in thought, then headed back toward the propeller rationalizing that all the damage would have to be back in that area. I remembered that the sub seemed off kilter after the crash, with the nose slightly down. Perhaps some part of her had been knocked loose to make us lose our balance that way. Every crucial, functioning part of the stern looked pristine. I decided to examine the secondary equipment whose parts weren't used for locomotion, starting with the jettison tray.

A jettison tray was a drop weight that was standard equipment on virtually all manned submersibles. It had two functions. First, it was used as ballast and secondly, as an emergency apparatus. On the Perry Class submersibles I operated, the tray was an 800 pounds of lead diving weights that was held in place by stainless steel pins. Should a pilot's power source ever fail, or if for any other reason he needed to surface in a hurry, he simply pulled a handle inside the cabin which dropped the weight, and the sub became instantly lighter and floated to the surface. I realized that the tray was in the exact spot where the sub had likely been hit, but I hadn't looked at it before because I'd been so concerned with the hull and moving parts. Now, I got down on all fours to examine it.

"Bloody hell," I whispered to myself, sitting down on the deck in disbelief. The jettison tray, all 800 pounds of it, had been knocked past one of its release pins and was jammed in place. Whatever had hit us, had rushed us with a force strong enough to break 800 pounds of metal free from its secure position.

I had no idea what kind of an animal could cause such damage and then just disappear into the abyss without a trace, but whatever it was, I knew one thing for sure. I was going to get the predator on film. The only question was how.

2

The sea monster would not let me be. I had tried to stop thinking about what kind of animal could have hit my sub a few days ago, but forcing myself to forget was as useless as it was exhausting. The animal might have glanced off the sub with the speed of a ricocheting bullet, but still it lingered, endlessly prowling my imagination. It had always been my experience that it was never what a man knew that was his undoing. It was what he didn't know that got him in the end. That fear of the unknown was keeping me from letting the moment pass away as it should. Trying with all my might to relax, a technique that never seemed to work, I had actually managed to spread out in a hammock with a book and a cold drink on my day off. My choice of reading material, however, could not have been worse. I was reading about accidental encounters with sea life in Alvin, the workhorse submersible for Woods Hole Oceanographic Institute.

Alvin is a very famous manned submarine, just a few feet longer than the subs I operated. It is probably best known for discovering the wreck of the Titanic back in 1985. In its celebrated forty-year career, this DSV (Deep Submergence Vehicle) has had more than a few encounters with large marine life and one face-off in particular caught my eye. During dive number 202 on July 6th, 1967, an angry swordfish decided to attack Alvin at a depth of 2000 feet. Apparently, the fish was unhappy at the breach of its territory by the mechanical thing and it rammed the sub with all its might, wedging its sword firmly in a crevice between the skin of the passenger compartment and a bar on the outer frame. The furious fish was trapped and it struggled with all its might to break itself free, leaving a sizeable bloodstain on the ship's hull, but it was all in vain. Eventually, the swordfish died, was brought back to the surface, removed, and eaten with drawn butter and a lemon wedge.

After reading this fact, I caught myself smiling and downplayed my incident with the unknown force. It was probably wise to pass on the unlikely Giant Squid Theory, and consider something a little more "obvious" as an explanation. Perhaps it was a swordfish that had hit us too. The possibility was real enough. Swordfish loved the tropical waters around my beloved "George Town rectangle," but still, I couldn't shake the feeling that no swordfish I'd ever seen in these waters was big enough to move an 800 lb weight from its release pins. Some rare swordfish do grow quite large, but because of worldwide over fishing, the average weight of a swordfish in the Caribbean has gone from 300-400 pounds, down to around 150 pounds or less in the past few decades. Besides, it felt more like a whale than a swordfish that rammed us that day, although why and how a whale would attack my sub like that was beyond my comprehension.

I looked out to sea from the hammock where I was lying, and thought for a few moments about man's odd need to populate the sea with monsters. Tales of fantastic beasts were an understandable reaction to the very real, but still mind-boggling, phenomena that sailors and wave watchers had always encountered in the deep, and I suspected that virtually all these tall tales had a very similar origin:

Imagine for a moment, that you are a wholly uneducated farm boy from the 15th century. Like all farm boys since the dawn of time, you find yourself swinging a stick-sword in the garden and dreaming of slaying dragons, longing for adventure far beyond your little town. About the age of fifteen or so, you come to the unavoidable conclusion that, obviously, you are nothing like your friends and neighbors. All of them seem far too willing to resign themselves to this meager existence, with its long shifts of sunup to sundown, and days filled with backbreaking labor barely scratching a living out of the rocky soil. For someone with your unmistakable gifts to endure a future as bleak as that would be a travesty. You are a special one, restless to a fault, and far more ambitious than any of the other local farmboys. Steeped in such self-awareness, you feel confident as you sign on for a once-in-a-lifetime maritime expedition into uncharted territories with a royalty endorsed explorer who has lately been the talk of your village. A tall, suave man with an Italian last name that sounds like Columbo or Vespucci. His smaller, fast-talking assistant has told you all about the coming voyage and how it was expected to be the adventure of a lifetime. A man of your quality, he'd said, should not miss out on this opportunity.

Although you cannot possibly understand what adventures lay in store for you, you are more than eager to put your "X" on the contract held out to you. In your world, there have been no elementary classes in marine biology, no National Geographic Society nor Discovery Channel, and no Public Television bringing pictures of the monsters that lurk in the deep right into your little thatched cottage via TV. All you know of the world is contained in the twenty square miles that surround your farm. The words "whale," "squid," and "shark" are meaningless to you but, as you wave goodbye to your weeping Mama, cheerfully swinging your sea bag over your shoulder, you eagerly board the ship that will carry you to "the new world", fully believing that you understand this world better than most. You may not be able to read or write, but you are certain, to your soul's cove that the expedition you are about to embark on will make all the difference in your personal destiny.

Several days into the voyage, miserable with sunburn and dehydration, and dreaming about the paradise that was once your home; you are awakened from a deep sleep by an unusual, high-pitched sound outside your wooden ship. The sleep of your shipmates has been disturbed as well, and you pick up your cloaks to rush up on deck to see what could be causing the squealing commotion. Leaning over the side of 70-foot vessel, you notice that the surface of the sea seems to be boiling alongside the boat. In the moonlit waters, you can just make out a huge shadow below the surface, a shadow nearly as long as the ship itself and you excitedly point it out to the crew. You all watch it and agree; something gigantic is swimming beside your craft, matching its speed knot for knot, and disturbing the swells that pound against it. It is a Leviathan; a living thing of a size never before seen by anyone from dry land and although the creature follows the ship for a time, it suddenly turns away, vanishing into nothingness like a morning mist on the vineyards back home. Squinting, you stare out into the darkness, hoping to catch another glimpse of the thing, and wondering if your eyes have been playing tricks on you. Perhaps there wasn't anything out there after all. You see and hear only the lapping of the waves and the creaking wooden hull of the boat.

Then, in a tremendous snort, a geyser of hot air unexpectedly shoots out of the water next to the boat, and your whole skin flinches, your breath completely taken away. You see what appears to be a fountain of vapor spray, much like the fountain in the town square of your village, only this fountainhead is right in the middle of this godforsaken stretch of sea. What kind of an animal could create such a display, you wonder. Could it be a dragon?

The shadow dips again and suddenly, a monster of tremendous size breaches the water, shooting straight up into the air and flopping back down in tremendous splash, soaking everyone on the ship. Salt spray blinds you, and you are thunderstruck. If you are lucky enough to survive the rickets and scurvy of this trip, you know you will return home forever changed. Right there and then, you make a silent vow to yourself to tell everyone who will listen to you about the monster you have just seen. This is a moment far too important to live through only once.

As the days of your life pass, you are true to your word and you tell your story everywhere, although the tale grows taller from tavern to tavern. Wide-eyed children and grandchildren who listened in rapt attention to your adventures when they were young will eventually grow old and grizzled themselves, telling their own wide-eyed children all about the fire breathing, spiked, sea dragon Great Grandpa once encountered in the middle of the deep blue sea.

That is how sea monsters are born, and without a doubt, how they will survive. The pure enigma of the sea's depth ensures their immortality.

But I suppose we also created these entities in our imaginations because we have yet to shake that ancient "fight or flight" instinct that was a genetic remnant from the days when there really was something to fear from the animals around us. Today, the same adrenaline jolt that once fueled our ancestors escape from a charging Tyrannosaurus now kicked in as a Woody Allen-esque panic attack whenever some aggressive driver cuts us off on the freeway. Simply put, we were hereditarily programmed to freak out. Unfortunately, in the soft, cool comforts of the modern world, there was nowhere legitimate, except for socially sanctioned outlets like the cutthroat competition of the corporate world or the "anything goes" atmosphere of Las Vegas, for our basest instincts to be acceptably deployed. It was a deep-seated physical requirement to experience and release fear every now and again. It sends us to horror movies, puts us in fast cars, or recklessly draws us to extreme sports. The inherent need for fear was probably also the reason why so many of the lithographs of sea monsters from days long gone had very human-looking faces. Then, as now, the worst monsters dwelled within our own skins. The craving for "things that go bump in the night" accounted for our steadfast refusal to give up the search for many famous "monsters" long after their existence had been debunked. Creatures like Big Foot, Yeti, or the Loch Ness monster.

Although not technically a sea monster, Nessie, as the Loch Ness' most famous "resident" was known, is adored throughout the world. No one could dispute the fact that she was a very appealing looking apparition. With her long neck and soft flippers, she may well be considered the Audrey Hepburn of Cryptozoology. She charmed us physically, touching our hearts and seizing on our longing to see a dinosaur, in this case, a plesiosaur, turning what fossil fact clearly tells us was a fierce, toothsome brute, into a cute and cuddly, paddle-toy of a critter. Unseen by anyone whose story could possibly be substantiated, she was completely unknowable and yet, her very name called to mind an image that was as instantly recognizable as the Coca Cola trademark. Nessie was the perfect symbol of how man used his imagination and remarkable gift for rationalization to conquer his enduring ignorance and fear of the natural world. To add a cherry to the top of her many other delights, the Loch Ness Monster was also a full-on cash cow to the people around the community where she lived. Books and toys, plastic and bronze plesiosaurs, as well as DVDs of documentaries that either proved or debunked her existence, rake in countless Scottish tourist dollars annually, keeping many of her neighbors economically afloat. With all these sterling qualities, it seemed to me that the creature of Loch Ness wasn't really much of a "monster" after all. In fact, the only real downside to Nessie was that there was not one iota of credible evidence to be found anywhere that she actually existed. All sightings to date have either turned out to be unsupported legend or famous hoaxes, like the celebrated "surgeon's photograph" taken in the 1930's which was ultimately revealed to be a foot long model of the monster that was photographed by the fraud's perpetrators, then hastily stomped-on because the pranksters feared being caught. A deathbed confession by Christian Spurling, the photographer of the duplicitous trio, laid the hoax to rest in 1993.

Rest assured, however, there were real live monsters to be found in the depths of the sea. Not cute and cuddly fantasies like Nessie, but blood curdling, breathing, hideous creatures. Animals so gruesome, people are compelled to look away from their images with the same revulsion experienced when looking at pictures of cankers in a medical text. People simply didn't want to know that such things existed. But no matter how much we wanted to avoid the harsh "kill or be killed world" of the deep, it was nonetheless a fact that this inky hell existed. One of its inhabitants, a very large and aggressive one, had damn near bit a hole in my submarine.

I sat up in the hammock, dangled my legs over the side and scooted my feet into the flip-flops that were waiting for me in the grass. I couldn't rest. I decided to fill up my backpack with books and notepad and head out to the internet café' at PD's Pub, and finally figure out which of the creatures that lived in the deep was responsible for knocking that damn drop plate off its bolts. To ensure a clear head, I would walk.

There weren't many places as nicely suited to a sunny morning walkabout as George Town Harbor. It was a striking combination of white clapboard and green swaying palms set against blue sky on one street. Sitting directly across from steel and glass bank buildings on another. Near Fort George, it could seem for a moment as if time were standing smack in the middle of the 1700's, but just stroll up the road and around the bend, and time will be solidly back in the present. Grabbing an espresso or looking at Avant Garde art in some shopping gallery window near Pantonville. Effortlessly mixing the past with the present this way was a bit a specialty on the Cayman Islands, and something that was wholly ingrained in the day-to-day lives of the locals. Caymanians were a group of casual, but conservative, individuals with charming West Indian accents. Although tremendously multi-ethnic in origin, they were nonetheless fully respectful of one another's ways and customs. There might have been laws on the books here forbidding witchcraft, voodoo, astrology and palm reading for years in order to satisfy the early missionary residents, but even so, practitioners of Christianity and Voodoo lived peacefully side-by-side, adapting to and sometimes even embracing each other's ways. Many of the locals came from families that had called these tiny islands home for centuries. So rooted was the community here in fact, that a huge segment of the population actually shared a common surname. At least once every fifteen minutes a traveler will, without question, run into someone by the name of Bodden.

Around the time of the American Revolution, when less than 400 people inhabited the south side of Grand Cayman, the most prominent family of that paradisiacal space and time was the Boddens. William Bodden, descendant of the first resident known to carry that name, was a man now poetically referred to as "the Grahnd Old MAHN of Grahnd CAY-mahn."

William was the chief magistrate and head of the militia here from 1798 until his death in 1823. It was he who built the first roads and churches and established the first shipbuilding sites on the island. Most famously however, it was William Bodden, or at least someone in his extended household, who was apparently quite irresistible to the ladies. By 1773, little offspring named Bodden had begun cropping up all over the island like freckles in the sunshine. According to a Royal Navy survey of that date:

"There are 21 [families named Bodden] at the SouthSide, which we have called BoddenTown, 13 at the West End, commonly called Hogsties, 3 at the East End, and 2 at Spot's Bay, in all 39 families"

That was out of around 70 families total. Today it seemed to me at least that one out of every three people on Grand Cayman were part of the Bodden clan. If last names counted for anything, William Bodden wasn't just a figurative father of Cayman Islands, he was also one of the principal biological fathers as well. To avoid confusion, locals frequently referred to one another only by a title and first name, as in Mr. Jim or Miss Sally, leaving the last name presumptive.

I was reminded again of the importance of the Boddens as I passed the statue of James Manoah Bodden, on my way to the pub. James Manoah was another Bodden who had truly earned his place of honor in Cayman history by establishing an airport here in 1953. While that may not sound like a huge accomplishment to those of us who enjoy easy and affordable transportation on the mainland, to the water-bound people of Grand Cayman, it was an achievement that has yet to be equaled. With the coming of a public airport, ordinary residents were finally able to get the hell off of the island whenever they had the inclination and the cash to do so. Grand Cayman may be beautiful, but one can only imagine the island fever suffered here before the days of air travel. For this achievement, J.M. Bodden became the Cayman Island's first official National Hero.

Of all the Boddens who had left their imprint on this island however, perhaps the most charming and appropriate legacy was the one left by Captain Rayal B. Bodden. Captain Rayal, like many of his ancestors, was a ship builder, building his first rig when he was only 14. His young age attested to the fact that he was something of a draftsman/prodigy whose talents could scarcely be contained in the building of ships alone. In the 1920's Rayall also hung up a shingle as a land-based architect.

Immediately, and solely on the basis of his outstanding reputation as a ship builder, Captain Bodden was commissioned to design many of George Town's most prominent public buildings. Pick up any postcard in George Town today and it would probably feature a sample of his work. He designed the Town Hall, the Elmslie Memorial Church, the General Post Office, and the Public Library. All of these structures were pure Caribbean, painted white as bone, perhaps a bit primitive in construction by continental standards. Flawlessly capturing the breezy, barefoot, tropical feel of island life. Every one of them was shaped, in one form or another, exactly like the ships Captain Rayal was so famous for building. The roof of the library, for example, was shaped like a ship's hull, turned upside down, in homage to the many wrecks that lay in the silent depths of the local harbor. A similar roof covered the

Church, and the Post Office was designed with a ship's distinctive timberwork exposed in the interior. Mailing a letter in rough weather there, the building is almost expected to start pitching with the swells. It seemed that Rayal Bodden's architecture, like the island of Grand Cayman itself, could never quite escape the dominion of the sea. The blue Caribbean ruled the collective consciousness here, and I understood the Captain's obsession perfectly. At that moment, the sea and its creatures had quite a stranglehold on me as well.

I stopped into the bookstore next to PD's on Seven Mile Beach to see if they had any titles that could help my search. The best place to start any sort of research was with the indisputable facts of a case, so I searched the volumes for titles about local sea life, silently ticking off a checklist of the details I knew to be certain about the attack in my mind. Whatever had hit us was big. That was fact one. Big enough to rock the sub and bend the drop plate anyway. Fact two, the animal was either wickedly fast or extremely stealthy, because in the time it took for me to regain my composure and look out to see what hit us, it vanished. Very few living beings can move that fast. Fact three, it had to be a living thing, or at the very least, a traveling object, because whatever it was, it rammed the sub upwards, from beneath, where I knew there was nothing but 5000 feet of canyon and water. And the fourth, most significant fact of all was that the attack happened in my own personal "George Town Rectangle." That meant it had to be something that was native to that bizarre area. I whispered the list to myself, "Something large, something fast, something stealthy, and something native."

That narrowed my research options nicely. I enlisted the help of a clerk, whose nametag identified him as a Mr. Bodden, and collected my selections.

One large, fast, sea dweller who travels often through the Caribbean was the Whale. Grand Cayman lay well within the migratory routes of several species including the Sperm whale, the Blue, the Fin, the Right, Humpback, and Minike whales. It certainly seemed possible that one of these giants could have been responsible for hitting the sub that day. Just recently in fact, I'd heard that a group of divers had discovered multiple pods of Sperm Whales playing off the coast of Cayman Brac and they actually got to jump in and swim with them. Apparently Mr. Bodden, the clerk, had heard about this incident too, and he told me that there was an entire website dedicated to the occasion, directing me next door to the pub's Internet station, a precious commodity in this part of the world. Because he recognized my employer's name on my cap, he suggested I go ahead and take a few books with me to the pub while I did my research, reminding me politely to be sure and return the ones I didn't want to buy. It was an offer I gladly accepted. I selected a few titles on Whale, Squid and Sharks, and with a grateful nod, backed out the door saying I'd be back as soon as I could. At PD's, I ordered a cup of coffee, settled in at a keyboard, and typed in the address Mr. Bodden had given me. My face lit up from the computer glow and the information on the site. Using photos and description, the webmaster explained how he and a group of diving buddies had watched the whales for a couple of hours, snapping the pictures of the animals as they surfaced, and timing them as they plummeted into the 5000 foot trench, returning every ten minutes. After being sure of their position and behavior, he and his friends donned some snorkeling gear and hopped in to join them. Imagine how small and insignificant they must have felt using swim fins to paddle next to a 30-foot mother and her 15-foot calf in the endless expanse of the sea. Suddenly, I felt a swell of plausibility go through me. Without question, a Sperm Whale rocketing up from 5000 feet on a quest for air was more than missile enough to cause the damage my sub had sustained. The trouble was, any creature the size of a soaring Sperm Whale would have done much worse damage than just knocking one lousy drop plate off the sub should he have smacked into me. That kind of impact would've packed enough G's to turn my brain to Jello.

So maybe it wasn't a Sperm Whale then, but one of the smaller whale species that bumped us. Once again though, I had to contend with the fact that whales in general were just not aggressive with people or their machines as a rule, and would probably not randomly attack a sub. Perhaps some playful whale calf might have seen the sub as a shiny yellow plaything though, or a small whale might have been disoriented and ran into us accidentally, but I doubted it. I picked up Richard Ellis' book, Monsters of the Sea and starting reading about whales to see what I could find out to add to my list of facts about these remarkable animals.

Although these days, men see whales, particularly those who sport the plankton-catching baleen instead of teeth, as gentle giants, this was a fairly recent understanding. For hundreds of years, whales were thought to be bloodthirsty flesh-eaters, eager to attack ships, swallowing their peg-legged, parrot-toting sailor-contents whole: utterly evil predators who were deserving of any fate set upon them. Whales, along with the Giant Squid, were the basis for most of the original sea monster

legends that endured. Look no farther than Moby Dick to get
an idea of the devil-fish mythology we managed to create
around the Leviathan. Small wonder we misunderstood them
so completely too, because the secret world of the Whale was,
and still is, all but invisible to man. Whales spend their days
diving and hiding, surfacing only long enough to shock and
amaze us. Until fairly recently, we knew virtually nothing
about their habits, so we made up terrifying stories about them
to explain their behaviors, as people often do when faced
with frightening individuals they do not understand.
According to Ellis, "free swimming whales were not [even]
photographed until 1975."

Then, in the early 1970s, the ghastly statistics of the whaling
industry were made public for the first time. Ellis says, "people
were killing whales in staggering numbers- (with) the quota
for Sperm Whales in the North Pacific for 1973 (set at) 10,703."
Faced with such gruesome information, humankind suddenly
began to care about the fate of the rapidly vanishing whale
and in turn, about the fate of the dying seas. The creature's
genocide, and the outrage it engendered, was the very beginning
of the "Save the Whales" movement, and quicker than you
can say "Greenpeace," the once hated whale was a new
environmental hero who ushered in a different age, a world
where recycling and ecological responsibility ruled.

Ironically, it was a Killer Whale named Namu who played the
most pivotal role in this shifting perception of whales. Killer
Whales were not the "gentle giants" its cousins were considered
to be. An Orca might be beautiful and clever, but make no
mistake; they have earned the first part of their name the
hard way. They were nearly as murderous as Melville imagined

his White Whale to be, killing bigger whales without compunction. A pod of Orcas will gleefully separate a frantic Gray Whale mother from her calf, and repeatedly butt the calf to death as the mother tries in vain to support her child from beneath and save its life. Once the grieving mother was finally herded to the side, the Orcas would feed on the calf's carcass, along with any other sea creature that would make a good, chewy mouthful, then be on their guilt-free way. As to the second half of their name, a Killer Whale was not a whale at all, but actually the largest member of the dolphin family. It was believed that their current name might have been a bastardization of an ancient phrase that meant "Killer of Whales." In 1965, an Orca called Namu was accidentally caught inside a fishing net, rescued, hand fed and trained over time by his captors until ultimately, he was transformed into a Flipper-style entertainer who became a big enough draw to have an entire theme park built around him. It was a genuine Hollywood fairy tale, but with a curiously twisted ending. After spending an eternity shrouded in mystery, the heavens aligned for one glorious moment, and in the form of a glistening black and white murderous Killer Whale, who wasn't even a whale at all, suddenly, the whale became the Mahatma Gandhi of the Sea. Seemingly overnight, Humpbacks made record albums and graced magazine covers, contrite humans stopped harpooning whales and started studying their language instead, and schoolchildren collected pennies in order to free Willy. The gears of an earnest and positive publicity machine for the conservation of the seas had been set fully into motion and they were still chugging along today. It was safe to say that the formerly relived whale had done more for the restoration of our damaged oceans than even the most skilled environmental scientists. Today, we've not only made great strides in saving the Whale, it seemed that by using its natural charisma to focus human attention on the importance of the marine ecosystem to the planet's survival, the whale has attempted to save our us as well.

The question remained however. "Will whales attack a ship?" Under the right circumstances, it seemed that the answer was yes. There were many politically incorrect stories about whales the public probably won't ever hear. In a show in San Diego's Sea World one summer afternoon in 1989 for example, a captive Killer Whale who was the mother of a new calf, nearly injured a trainer and angrily butted a cast mate, killing herself in the process and changing the arena's aqua-blue water to a murky blood red in front of a full arena of horrified onlookers. There was a recent news story about a whale hunter from Alaska who was slapped by the tail of a harpooned Gray Whale and later found dead and bleeding from the ears, but it was nowhere near as familiar as the stories of Gray Whales rising up by whale watching boats for a quick back-scratch and a bit of admiration from the people on board. While it is true that whales were gentle animals, usually, and that they do not kill, without provocation, it was also important to remember that they were not philosophers, musicians nor angels. They were simply very big, breathtaking animals who deserved to live unencumbered in freedom and safety. Once encountered, they were never to be forgotten. The fact that my sub's attacker was a stealthy fellow, sneaky enough to hit and run while remaining unseen, meant that I probably had to rule out a whale as the creature who had attacked my ship. It was not only unlikely that a whale would attack any submarine for no good reason; it was just very hard to hide a whale.

My mind went back to the Kraken, the mysterious living sea monster. Even though the existence of this giant species of squid had now been proven beyond a doubt through the examination of beached specimens, it had nonetheless been extraordinarily hard for the Giant Squid, Archituethis, to shake his mythical "sea serpent" image. Besides the fact that a living specimen of Giant Squid had never been captured, there had simply been far too many stories told for far too many years about the terrible Kraken, the polyp-shaped fiend who grabbed ships by the mast and capsized them, feasting on their inhabitants with a huge, hooked beak. In some versions of this tale, the Kraken had even been the possessor of ten distinct heads. In Twenty Thousand Leagues Under the Sea, the Giant Squid was described by Jules Verne a "A whim of nature" with a tongue "made of a hornlike substance and armed with several rows of sharp teeth [that would] come out and shake what seemed like veritable cutlery." It was "a terrible monster, worthy of all the legends about such creatures." Most of these stories, obviously, are nonsense, but not every account passed down from generation to generation about the aggressiveness of the Giant Squid has turned out to be baloney. According to Michel Bright's 1989 book, There Are Giants in the Sea, at least one Architheuthis really did attack a ship in the twentieth century and pretty convincing evidence of the attack was collected at the site. Skeptics are advised to "hearken to [this] sobering tale of the Brunswick."

In the early 1930s, a 500 foot auxiliary tanker called Brunswick was sailing from Hawaii to Samoa in the Pacific, when her Commander, Arne Grooningstaeter of the Royal Norwegian Navy, could have sworn he saw a squid about 30 feet in length, not counting the 30 or more feet of tentacles trailing

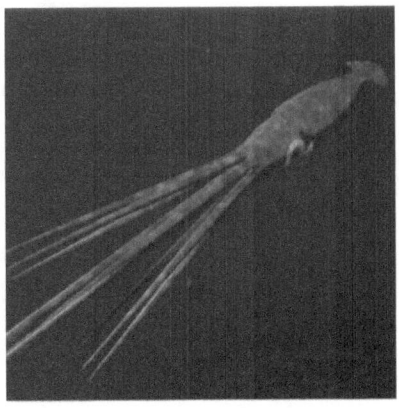

behind it, breaking the water's surface at the stern of his ship. It was an unusual sighting to say the least. Raising a pair of binoculars to his eyes, he looked at the animal, cleaned the lenses, and looked again, sketching exactly what he'd seen in his ship's log. After a detailed consultation with other members of the crew, there was little doubt about it. Giant Squid, a group of them, were actually chasing his vessel. The ship steered away and sped up to avoid the animals, but the Squids' tenacity in their pursuit made it impossible to shake them. In no time, the animals managed to catch up to the ship and one of them began to repeatedly slam its body against the side, fascinating and terrifying the crew. On the third slam, one animal reached up with a mighty tentacle, about ten inches or so in diameter, and actually tried to fasten itself to the side, but the metal hull proved too smooth to latch onto, and the squid slid away. The crew stood silently on deck, watching with open mouths as undaunted, the determined pack of Architeuthis simply dropped back towards the stern and tried to take another run at their prey. This time however, when the most aggressive of the animals threw its weight against the ship, the Squid found the propeller blades and was immediately hacked to bits. Incredulous at the half-mile long trail of blood that followed his vessel, the Captain promptly recorded the incident, in fully gruesome detail, in his ship's log.

That an attack like this could happen even once was extraordinary enough, but the fact that the very same ship was attacked three times without retreat, made the event significant to 1930's scientists. Prior to the Brunswick incident, it was assumed that in the battle between Sperm Whale and Archituethis, it was the Sperm Whale who was always the aggressor. The whale was the one who was frequently found with a belly full of calamari while all the Squid specimens' bellies showed nothing but a painful growl where digested food should be. This attack meant that the established food chain relationship with the whale as predator and Arcitheuthis as prey might not be set in stone after all. Perhaps the Brunswick was attacked because it was traveling at about 12 knots, a speed very similar those clocked by Sperm Whale hunters when chasing prey in the open ocean. And, perhaps, Squid bellies are always found empty because they have a ridiculously effective and speedy digestive system in order to make short work of a consumed Sperm Whale. Whatever the real cause of the attack, there is no doubt that these particular giant squid meant to attack and down the huge, metal Brunswick. probably to make a meal.

I put the book down, and got up to get a refill on my cup of coffee. At last, I knew for a fact that Architeuthis was large enough to attack the sub, strong enough to do the damage that was done, and at 12 knots traveling speed to my ship's paltry seven, certainly fast enough to hit us and get away unseen. Virtually everything a Giant Squid did, he did unseen. But I still didn't know how I could be sure that Arcituethis lived anywhere near the George Town Rectangle. The answer, naturally, was that I couldn't be sure, but maybe I could make an educated guess at the probability with just a little more information. I added cream, stirred my cup, and returned to my station to see what more I could find out about the known habitats of Giant Squid.

Nearly all of the bodies of Architeuthis have been found in one of a very few locations: near Newfoundland, Britain, or Scandinavia. The water in all those places was very cold, causing marine biologists to speculate that the Kraken preferred icy waters. There were even some theorists who suggest that it was a sudden rise in water temperature in those locations, where occasionally, warmer waters will meet Arctic ones, that were the cause of the huge Squid dying and washing up on shore in the first place.

I looked out the window of the library in the direction of the warm Cayman shore. One thing was certain. If Giant Squid really did need cooler water to survive, then none of them were likely to live in the Caribbean. Reading on, however, I discovered that there have also been specimens, or at least digested bits of specimens, discovered in the warmer waters off of Nambia, Brazil, and California, and there was even a single juvenile specimen found inside a Lancetfish in fully tropical waters. Now to me, that said more about the migratory power of a Lancetfish than it did about the squid's preferred habitat, but in In The Search for the Giant Squid, Richard Ellis proposed a different explanation. He said that a group of Russian Scientists had developed a theory that Architeuthis actually traveled the entire length of the globe in its lifespan. Breeding in subtropical waters, spending their youth in the warmer, tropical seas, and finally heading upwards to feed and grow huge on the abundance of food in the cold northern oceans. In other words, depending on the age of the animal, and whether or not it was in spawning mode, they lived absolutely everywhere on earth.

I closed the book and sighed. Even with all the books in the world and the fastest internet connection known to man, I wasn't going to be able to find enough hard evidence to conclude that a Giant Squid was the animal that hit me. The chances of an attack by an animal as rarely encountered as an Atchiteuthis were astronomical, and if I was going to fully rule out whale and Giant Squid, that left me only one other local creature who was large enough to cause the sort of damage my sub had incurred. It must have been a shark.

There were several species of shark that called the George Town rectangle their home. Nearly all of them are gentle fish, much more inclined to run away from a sub than toward it. Take the Nurse Shark for example. Many a terrified Caribbean diver had loaded his wet suit stumbling across a school of 10-foot Nurse Sharks milling about in a "sharky" cocktail party in local waters, but there was no need for panic. Unless provoked by extraordinary circumstances, a Nurse Shark would almost never attack a human. The Caribbean Reef Shark, another sizeable set of jaws that inhabited the rectangle, might be drawn to divers with twinkling jewelry, but there were very few records of them attacking anyone who wore it. And, although there had been sightings of the largest shark in the entire world, in fact, the largest animal (non mammal) found anywhere on this planet, it was unlikely that the wholly non-aggressive Whale Shark was the animal that struck my sub. There is no quieter, less aggressive creature swimming the sea today.

Still, I could not deny that a Whale Shark had all the physiological elements necessary to cause the damage we sustained. Unlike Nurse Sharks who linger about at 250 feet and Reef Sharks who have only been found as deep as 98 feet, a Whale Shark actually goes deep enough to have met the sub where we were lying that day, at 1200 feet. And because these Goliaths grow up to 50 feet in length, they were certainly large enough to have smashed that drop plate and more. But the truth was, no Whale Shark had ever been seen attacking anything other than plankton or fish spawn, period. They just didn't have the kind of teeth or temperament a fish needed for violence. A Whale Shark was so gentle in fact that whenever divers were lucky enough to encounter one, they were free to clamber all over the shark's huge back as he swims on helplessly, parasites in tow. When the animal has had enough of the attention, he only sinks down farther in the water, like a cowering child trying to ditch a bully.

The Whale Shark was a favorite subject of early sea monster storytellers because of its tremendous size and gaping mouth, which was approximately the size of an opened doorway. Spread wide and swimming by, speckled lips flapping against the current, a Whale Shark's mouth looked as if he was trying to swallow the entire sea in one gulp. Monstrous though he might seem, a Whale Shark would never have hit my sub, even accidentally, and if he had, he still would not have been able to slip away unseen. The top speed of this animal was 3 MPH.

Great Whites did not normally inhabit these waters, thankfully. In fact, the only real people biters that made their home here were Tiger and Hammerhead sharks. Ordinarily, Hammerheads would remain out of sight and pose no threat to divers at all, but in recent past, a dive operator came up with the idea of promoting shark feeding "thrill dives." On these excursions, people, for reasons best known to themselves, boat out into the waters off the East end of the Island and there, a "baiter" in chain mail and a bucket of chum will hop into the water and spread the scent all around. When hungry sharks arrive, the other divers could enjoy a brisk swim, dodging the flashing teeth of the usually docile Hammerhead and Reef Sharks. Although it might seem that a program like this one would ultimately be destined to failure as its practitioners systematically become shark food, the Cayman Islands authorities didn't wait for that to happen. They cracked down on the practice, hard. Before the first missing limb could be reported, the fine for this practice was established at $500,000, followed by six months in jail, and mandatory confiscation of the vessel. Needless to say, it was a practice that quickly ceased.

All things considered, it seemed that there was only one local species that seemed to have it all, the motive, means, and the opportunity, to be my sub's assailant: the Giant Six-gill shark.

There was at least one Six-gill shark, around 20 feet long, who lived in the inky blackness of the deepest trenches in the Caribbean. There, it moved as silently and as deftly as a stealth missile. We only knew this giant existed because in the 1980's, a National Geographic team was fortunate enough to had seen it. It could be hard to visualize just how tremendous a twenty-foot shark really was, but such a fish would be approximately as long as the average two-story house was tall and it would weigh about 2,000 pounds. Each one of its teeth, laying six rows deep, would be 2 inches long or about the length of your thumb, and although all sharks frequently lose teeth, a 20 foot Six-gill would lose literally tens of thousands of them in a lifetime; teeth that were spike-like on the top and saw-like on the lower jaw, that form a jagged trap so fierce it could snap a 60 pound tuna in half in one urgent bite. As one of these daggers falls out, another immediately takes its place, so a Six-gill was never without his weaponry.

We've only known for a fact that Six-gill sharks still existed in the twentieth century since the 1960's. It wasn't until then that specimens of this presumed-to-be-extinct animal were finally found, inexplicably tangled in fishing nets. Forced by some unknown power to rise from the safety of their ultra-deep homes and into dangerous contact with humans. The first couple of decades that followed this surprising discovery, there was plenty of anecdotal evidence, and even some live captures to feed our knowledge of the mysterious animal, but the most interesting feature of these sightings was the size of the fish, all between 8 and 14 feet in length, unusually large for a shark. By comparison, the average Great White grew to about 12-15 feet. One story even existed of a fishing crew in Scotland who allegedly caught a 26-foot Six-gill, and since that size was more in keeping with the fossil records of the extinct 40-foot Megalodon, Cryptozoologists who studied such sea monsters went wild with expectation. In true fish-story form though, it seemed that none of the Scottish fisherman who supposedly caught this giant Six-gill remembered to bring a camera and take a picture, so the rumor of the 26-footer was summarily discredited.

For many years, the longest Six-gill ever recorded was 15 and three quarters feet in length, which was a huge hunk of shark in its own right, but still nowhere near big enough to convince biologists that a colossal version of a primitive shark might still be roaming the seas. It took no less a scientific luminary than the Shark Lady, Dr. Eugenie Clark, a marine biologist with more than forty years of discoveries to her name, to prove that perhaps the 99% of the ocean we knew nothing about was, in fact, holding on to a big fish or two. During a project of the '80's, Dr. Clark was diving off the shore of Bermuda in the research submarine Pisces VI, baiting and filming Six-gills for a National Geographic documentary when, suddenly, a tremendous silhouette appeared in her viewport. The shark that curled around the sub and excited her beyond words was between 18 and 20 feet in length and a remarkable discovery; over three feet longer than it was previously believed a Six-gill could grow. The film she took was also irrefutable proof that at least one giant did still live among us.

Although filmed records like Dr. Clark's proved that this tremendous predator of the deepest ocean was still very much a part of the present, a Six-gill was still a living fossil, part of a group known as the primitive sharks about which we know very little. One thing we did know was that the fossilized dental remains of ancient six gills were almost identical to the Six Gill that swim the seas today. Apparently, they'd been with us, virtually unchanged, for almost 200 million years, from around the time of the Triassic era, well before the dinosaurs.

They swim deep, come up hard, and a twenty-foot Six-gill was easily beast enough to have blasted off that drop plate. But Dr. Clark's 20 footer was the only proven Giant Six-gill in Caribbean waters. It had only been seen once and then it was under extraordinary circumstances, lured by bait. I certainly hadn't been spreading chum around the day we were attacked, and I doubted that the smaller, much more common 8 to 12 footers who lived here could have caused the drop plate damage.

So it looked as if I was back to square one. It could have been a whale that bent the drop plate, but not likely. It could have been an Archeteuthis that hit us, but that would be one for the record books, not to mention completely impossible to prove. And it could have been the snap of a flesh-eating shark, but it would have to have been a shark of such a tremendous size that no one had ever seen anything like it before: three very unlikely scenarios. I chose one or two books to buy from the pile I had amassed, and returned my coffee mug to a bus tray, then went next door to Mr. Bodden who accepted my purchases and rejections with a knowing smile. We both knew that my answer would not be found here, among the books, but back down in the dark, silent, deep.

Walking home, I thought about another living sea monster whose very discovery took everyone by surprise. In 1976, a United States research vessel working off of the Hawaiian Islands was hauling in its anchors from the deep when the crew felt a tremendous drag on the lines. The anchors on this specialized ship were a parachute-like apparatus that kept the ship from drifting wherever the water was too deep for a conventional anchor. Apparently, it also made for perfect accidental bait and fishing line because, when the anchors were pulled fully upward, the sailors got the surprise of their life. There, dangling off the end was 1,650 pounds of flesh whose chief feature was an enormous, gaping, bioluminescent mouth with grand blubbery lips. It was a shark of some kind, 14 feet long, and freakish by anyone's standards. No living human had ever laid eyes on an animal like this in all the history of time. After a thorough examination at a nearby aquarium in Honolulu, it was decided that this shark was no killer, but a brand new species of plankton eater who, for obvious reasons, they decided to name Megachasma pelagios, or "Megamouth." The Megamouth shark was a creature that no one was looking for, nor even dreamed existed, and if that first captured specimen had not been myopic enough to mistake a parachute-anchor for a cloud of plankton in waters that were a mind-boggling 15,000 feet deep, it would likely never have been discovered at all. Miraculously though, it was, and the hope this discovery gave sea monster enthusiasts was infinite. After all, if the sea could hide a 14-foot, sea creature with an enormous glow-in-the-dark mouth for centuries, who knew what else might be lurking down there?

And that was the question that man had faced time and again. What is lurking down there? In spite of the harsh glare of meticulous scientific studies, as well as the more fanciful explanations offered by cryptozoologists, there had been no real answers to this puzzle even when the occasional jackpot of physical evidence happened to appear. There had been giant blobs of decaying animal tissue that had been found washed up on beaches all around the world. In the summer of 2003, for example, a mass of flesh about 12 meters long rolled onto a beach in Chile, and both scientists and true monster believers swarmed all over it like flies in the hot South American sun. The prevailing theory was that the pile of skin was probably a whale carcass, but just as in previous gobsters found in St. Augustine in 1896, in Tasmania in 1960, and in Bermuda in 1988, there was a huge rooting section who believed the remains would eventually be identified as a mythological Giant Octopus. In all other instances, no ultimate determination could be made about these mysterious gobs of tissue, but in the case of this Chilean Blob, a laboratory at the University of South Florida did DNA testing that proved it was nothing more than an exceedingly fetid corpse of a sperm whale. And so the debate rages on.

Arriving back at Sunset House, I put away my newly acquired books, and started making a tuna sandwich. The little tin of fish got me to thinking about all the changes in the world's oceans over the last hundred years or so. Not long ago, there were great schools of tuna roaming the sea, not only in the Caribbean, but everywhere around the world. Now, certain varieties are becoming harder and harder to find. According to John Seabrook in Death of a Giant: Stalking the Disappearing Bluefin Tuna in Harper's Magazine, June 1994:

" . . . The International Commission for the Conservation of Atlantic Tunas, an organization that monitors and tries to regulate the fishery, [says] the numbers of adult giant bluefin tuna in the western Atlantic Ocean have declined drastically since the mid-Seventies. A graph based on these figures looks like one of those charts of company earnings in business cartoons, with the head of the company perched on the window ledge about to jump out. On the left side of the graph, in the year 1970, the giant -tuna population is 220,000. On the right side of the graph, in the year 1990, the population has dropped nearly 90 percent and stands at less than 25,000.

Fishermen who are not much older than forty tell stories about the tremendous bounty of the sea in their youths, of swordfish playing off Montauk beach, of tuna blocking the breakwater at Provincetown. As recently as 1975 there was a near-coastal fishery for flounder off Cape Cod; hardly anyone catches a flounder there now. No one catches a halibut. More fishermen, more demand for seafood, and better technology for catching fish are the main reasons for these declines. The invention of loran, a navigational system that allows even the most unseafaring fisherman to know exactly where he is on the ocean at all times, has had a devastating effect on fish.

Whatever the reason, more and more animals from the abyss did seem to be vanishing these days. Those that survived were rising ever higher from their usually secure deep homes on a nightly hunt for scarce food supplies, and into contact with dangerous predators like man. Maybe that's why creatures like the Megamouth or the Coelacanth had only been seen for the first time in recent years. The Coelacanth was a famous fish, first found in 1938 off the coast of South Africa, caught in a fisherman's net. It was an odd looking fish with large, prehistoric-type scales and peculiar fins that stood out on stems. The trawler crew that found it was so taken aback by the curious appearance of the animal that they took it to a museum in East London and gave it directly to the curator there, Marjorie Courtney-Latimer, to see if she knew what it was. She realized instantly that this was no identifiable genus, so she preserved the specimen, and contacted a professor friend of hers at Rhodes University to help her identify the fish. Together, Courtney-Latimer and Prof. J.L.B. Smith discovered that this "new" fish was not a new animal at all, but nearly identical to fossils of Crossopterygii, an animal that had been extinct for over 70 million years. The stem-fins of the fossils of Crossopterygii had been presumed to be predecessors to land animal's more recently evolved limbs. In all probability, from the time of the dinosaur until that day in 1938, no human being had ever seen a Coelacanth, and yet, in the years that followed, numerous other specimens were subsequently caught and examined. Why were scarce fish, hidden so long by the dark waters of the sub sea trenches, suddenly being sighted? And if animals believed to be extinct, like the Coelacanth, or not even known to exist at all like the Megamouth Shark, were now surfacing from the absolute bowels of the sea, what else could we expect to find?

There was no doubt that the Holy Grail for Cryptozoologists and Marine Biologists alike would be the discovery of a living specimen of the Megalodon. The Megalodon, an ancient shark that was now presumed extinct, was 40 feet long, a length two times that of the Great White shark of Jaws fame. The phrase, "presumed extinct" was a carefully chosen one; because if the sea had taught us nothing else, it had proven that its dark depths could literally hide mountains, let alone Titanic-sized ships and even giant species never before seen. The fossilized teeth of the Megalodon were 6.5 inches long and just its smaller pectoral fin was the size of a tall man at 6 feet in length. These nightmarish monsters prospered 25 to 1.6 million years ago, and God only knew what force was big enough to finally cause them to become extinct. In fact, there were many who did not dare suggest that it was certain the

Megalodon was extinct. In Richard Ellis' book, Great White Shark for example, he stated that many scientists believed that this brute might have gone missing as recently as 10,000 years ago, a time frame that was the evolutionary blink of the eye. And although he did not hold with those who thought that an airplane-sized eating machine might still be swimming the abyss, he also said that, "except that we have not found one, there appears to be no reason why Megalodon should not be flourishing today."

There was one more unexplained phenomenon that might indicate at least one impossibly colossal beast was still swimming out of the sight and understanding of humankind right now. According to a CNN.com article of June 13th, 2002, scientists have recorded peculiar sounds "picked up by undersea microphones [and nicknamed the 'Bloop.']" The article says that, "While [the sound] bears the varying frequency hallmark of marine animals, it is far more powerful than the calls made by any creature known on earth . . . It is too big [even to be] a whale."

The Bloop was first picked up in 1997 by sensors planted throughout the world's oceans, a cold war attempt to spy on Soviet warships, a project that had accidentally proven invaluable in the study of marine life. The "Bloop" sounded very much like a hugely resonant version of a cartoon sound effect of water dripping, and was widely held to be biological in origin. An animal, larger than any known whale, making a noise that was loud enough to echo across the deep caverns of the sea was enough to give anyone pause. Unfortunately, even this tantalizing bit of data was just another unsolved mystery of the deep. The trouble with monsters was, they were almost impossible to find, difficult to study unless they were dead or mangled, and when live specimens were found, they had yet to be penned successfully. Most giant sea creatures died instantly without the ability to roam free, a characteristic that endeared them to the hearts of all men.

In other words, unless I found and filmed the animal that hit my sub myself, I would never know for certain what kind of "sea monster" I had run into.

I settled in with my innocuous looking sandwich, and taking a bite, realized that even tuna salad on white was a kind of predator-prey relationship in its own way. The ruthlessness that was the trademark of life in the sea certainly did not stop at the shoreline. Man and his need for food had as lasting an effect on the world's oceans as the mightiest of the Megalodon. I smiled at the powerful feeling this thought gave me. Then, I took another bite. My future was clear. For the remainder of my time in the Cayman Islands, I too, would be a predator, but not the kind of predator who mounted my next big catch on the wall. I was bringing my monster back on film.

3

A giant shark lurking in the local waters might seem like the ultimate in horror, but the greatest threat to man in the Cayman Islands was not a beast with razor sharp teeth or giant tentacles; it was the deceptively lovely azure waters of the Caribbean itself. The blue waves that surround all three islands cover some of the most treacherous, jagged, black reef in the world, and over the centuries hundreds, perhaps even thousands, of water craft of all shapes and sizes have stacked up on the pointy outcroppings. Some of these star-crossed ships, probably the ones whose Captains did something generous or kind in their lives, actually managed to limp back to shore intact. Just as often though, the wounded boats were simply gutted by the razor sharp reef, unceremoniously sunk, and reborn as breathtaking dive sites. My underwater collision with the giant creature had hardly been the only crash in this area. The sailor's loss had been the diver's gain time and again in Grand Cayman, generating magical undersea landscapes like the coral-loaded wreck of the Balboa, the breathtaking Carrie Lee, a favorite of tropical fish, and the remains of the marijuana-smuggling Oro Verde. While not technically a wreck, the Oro Verde was nonetheless a victim of a run-in, not with coral, but with the law. The ship was seized and sunk as a warning to other would-be criminals. It also looked as if it might make a fine artificial reef. It had indeed. The most famous of the Caymanian shipwrecks though, would have to be the spectacularly ill-fated "Wreck of the Ten Sails".

The story of this 10-ship pile up off the East End of Grand Cayman began on a very dark night in November during the late 1700's. That evening, the Captain of the Convert, a pilot ship in a fleet of sailing craft that traveled the trade route from Jamaica to Britain, ran his boat aground on one of the worst parts of the reef. He'd been unable to navigate successfully in the overcast night skies and, because there were no light-houses to steer by in those days, he was literally sailing blind in a sea of daggers. After it became apparent that his ship was sinking, the Captain ordered most of his men to abandon ship, except for a select few whom he asked to stay and send a signal to the other ships in the convoy, aiming to warn them away. If he could not save the lives of his own men he reasoned, perhaps he could save the lives of the men aboard the nine vessels sailing behind him. Sadly, the sailor who received the signal on the second ship was a little slow on the uptake that particular night. He may have been drinking, or more likely, he was just a young man who knew very little about maritime signage and misunderstood the urgent warning, interpreting it instead as a call to move closer to the pilot ship. It was a mistake he must have realized the moment he heard the horrible crackling of splintered wood as his ship ran aground. One by one, 10 full sized merchant ships junked themselves on top of the rocks and, ultimately, on top of each other only a short distance from shore.

The few inhabitants that were watching the disaster were quick to act. Summoning all the help they could gather from the paltry number of people who actually lived on the East End, they hopped into boats, some even wading in, and set out to rescue as many castaways as they could. Casualty statistics that exist from the Wreck of the Ten Sails vary, but they run a tight little gamut from a mere eight lives lost to no deaths reported at all. King George III was supposed to have been so thrilled about this minimal loss of life that he granted the islands freedom from taxation as a reward and, so the legend goes, that is the why the island's tax-free status came to be; a colorful explanation of how two of the most historically significant events in Caymanian history tie neatly together.

For all the fanciful details of this wreck, however, there was one point that is hard fact. It was far more than simple generosity of spirit that drove the rescuers out to sea that November night. Shipwrecks literally rained gold on the poverty-stricken settlers of Grand Cayman back in the 1700's. These were people living on an island without agricultural capabilities and with virtually no other means of support. A wreck meant new foods, wood for houses, clothes, furniture, cooking supplies, and even new residents for the towns. Many of the sailors who were washed ashore here, stayed here, charmed by the trade winds and the nearly indistinguishable blue horizon of sky and sea. In time, they too learned to pray to God for a new wreck when the bounty of the old wreck had run out. One could only imagine the wry glances exchanged by onlookers and the smiles on the settler's faces as ten fully loaded ships crashed within easy reach of their salvage operations. The party must have lasted for weeks and the population increased handily because of it.

But of all of the wrecks that had happened around Grand Cayman, there was only one that haunted my personal dreams. It was not a spectacular wreck, nor was it historically significant. But for me, it was life altering. It cemented my decision to become a deep sub pilot and filmmaker, and literally changed the way I saw the world of the deep. It all happened in the George Town Rectangle on January 9th, 1976.

In George Town Harbor where I worked, the occasional squall was nothing new. Maybe that's why no one was worried that morning when the wind began to whip the British and Caymanian flags in front of the old, white clapboard Courthouse that had stood watch over the port since the 1830's. This had all happened before. By early afternoon though, the storm began in earnest and, plainly, it was going to be a nasty one. Breakers hit the shoreline with a splattering show of strength and the palms along South Church Street all bent in unison from the wind. It was developing into a type of winter gale the locals call a Nor'wester. The severe nature of these particular fronts came from the fact that as a cold system blows in from the north, its frigid air and strong winds clashed head on with the warm tropical breeze of the Caribbean, making for a vicious storm that gathered strength very quickly. To be safe, a wise sailor secured his vessel at the first blast of cool northwest wind, and then, with one watchful eye towards his ship, waited out the worst of the storm comfortably cocooned in a warm, rummy haze at a nearby cafe. Nor'westers were dangerous business here because George Town Harbor was the only safe passage leading into or out of Grand Cayman. The days of praying for a wreck were long gone by the twentieth century. If that harbor was closed for any reason, such as the debris of a shipwreck, it could mean rationing, food shortages, or worse for the locals. One more boat fed to this stretch of hungry ocean probably wouldn't matter that much, were it not for the whole, unfortunate, blocked-harbor business, but since no one on the island was too keen on becoming a virtual prisoner, people began to worry plenty when The Kirk Pride starting banging on the dock and straining against it's lines that Friday morning.

At around 1:00 PM the storm was in full force and the ship's master, Byron Eubanks of The Kirk Pride Shipping Company, decided that someone had to do something. The order came in the form of staticky message across on the VHS radio.

"Kirk Pride. Kirk Pride. This is Port Authority. Do you copy?"

It was a call Capt. Shelby Hydes knew was coming, but didn't want to answer. He dreaded the idea of pulling his ship out into the rock-ridden harbor in 45 MPH winds but knew that, sure as hell, some genius among the higher ups was going to get the jitters in a storm this size and demand that the vessel be moved. If you asked him, there was more danger to the port if he backed out into the middle of that mess than if he stayed put, but he also knew that jobs as sweet as piloting this freighter to Florida just didn't come along every day. A quick show of hands among the few thousand residents of this tiny island would probably turn up any number of sailors who would be happy to take over his job should he choose to ignore orders. He did as he was asked.

He picked up the mouthpiece and pressed the reply button.

"Roger that," he replied evenly. "Will be underway momentarily."

Slamming the handset back down, he wished that, for once, the powers that be would take into full account the fact that every time a boat goes out, in good weather or bad, to fish or move cargo or even to carry passengers on a luxury liner, real men put their very real lives on the line to get the job done.

The order was to release all but a bow spring line and get the ship over to an area directly out from the old Pageant Beach Hotel, a pretty pastel colored inn that was one of the two original hotels on the Island. It wasn't far and Captain Hydes felt confident he could get the job done with a minimum of irritation. He knew every hazard in that port. With a sizeable crew aboard to help, he called his men to stations, cast off in the driving rain and started backing out into the water to find room to turn around. But as the ship pulled away from the dock, engines running in reverse, something went terribly wrong. Even on the shore, onlookers heard a harsh "thud," and it seemed that everything mechanical on the Kirk Pride had suddenly gone lifeless.

"Kirk Pride, Kirk Pride . . . Are you able to get under way?" asked the crackling voice on the VHF. "What is your situation?" The harbormaster sounded more irritated than worried, but, when there was no response to his radio message, he knew something was not right. He craned his neck and squinted his eyes to get a better look at the ship through his tiny office window. "What the hell are they doing out there?" he wondered out loud.

With its aging, air start engine, The Kirk Pride could be a real night mare to pilot, and the storm was only making it worse. All 498 tons of her were drifting without engine as the captain gave the all-stop order so he could throw the engines out of reverse and into forward to get underway. With this type of pneumatic system, even a momentary airlock can mean a complete loss of control, rather like driving a brake-less 40 ton semi truck on a downhill stretch of icy two-lane. Only the skill and strong arm of the truck driver, spinning the wheel for all he's worth stands between machine and disaster at such a moment. As the order was given to throw the engines into forward, the worst possible scenario played out. The engine's chugging stopped dead, and the only sounds that could be heard were the pelting rain and the howling of the wind through the halyards. The engine was frozen dead.

Without an engine, the powerless vessel was immediately caught in the storm driven current and started skidding across the surface of the water until its bowline safety harness stretched to the snapping point. From the instant it broke free, the Kirk Pride spun helplessly, stern moving away from the bow, spiraling out to sea.

The radio crackled its message again. "Kirk Pride, Kirk Pride, what is your situation? Repeat. What is your situation?"

As recently as January 7th, two days before, the ship's engineer had announced that the temporary airlock the engine's fuel lines had been experiencing was safely under control. Freshly off-loaded, the boat's crewmembers were so exhausted from the latest run and so eager for a good meal and a good woman that no one had bothered to run any tests to prove if the engine was again functional. Tests just didn't seem like a priority when shore time beckoned, and besides, everyone knew that The Kirk Pride's engineer was more than competent. He'd handled this situation at least a million times before. But as the ship twisted closer to the rocks, the mistake of choosing immediate gratification over safety checks became a little clearer. The repairs had left the engine depleted of pressure, offering only enough power for the back up maneuver. There was simply nothing left to move forward. The Kirk Pride was utterly out of control and the situation couldn't get much worse.

That's when the Kirk Pride ran onto the reef with a piercing screech, knocking First Mate Ronnie Bodden flat and sending him skidding across the wet deck. Gouged, but clear-headed, he stood up again in the pelting rain, fumbled around for a flashlight, and hurried down a hatch to survey the damage to the cargo hold. Away from the roar of the storm, in the vast, creaking payload that held nothing but a few stacks of lumber and darkness, he could hear an ominous hissing sound. Frantically, he fanned his beam of light around the dusty space to find its source. It didn't take long.

"God Almighty," he gasped, taking an incredulous step back from the illuminated pipe of water he found spewing into the ship. "Is that a hole?"

As the cuffs of Ronnie's denim pants grew dark and wet and sea salt stung the little scrapes on his ankles, he had the answer to that question at least. He looked at a crewmate in confusion and turned his palms upward. "What the hell happened?" he asked, "We were just backing up!"

Below the choppy surface was a 24,000-foot plunge over the Cayman Wall directly to the bottom of the Bartlett Deep, and the Kirk Pride was taking on water fast. Like any Captain worth a damn, Hydes was operating in complete denial, believing it was still possible to save his ship.

His crew, however, had other ideas.

"There is a hole down here the size of a tire and we're taking on too much water!" Bodden shouted from the hold. His voice went from panic to anger in a single sentence. "We're being overwhelmed! There aren't enough pumps on the whole stinkin' ship to fix this mess!"

Swells were rising and the bow of The Kirk Pride was bobbing on top of the water like a tub-toy, her midsection brutally beating against the cay. The obstinate Captain Hydes got Ronnie's message from below, but started a vain attempt to turn the ship away from the rock anyway. His freighter may have been only a quarter mile from shore, but it was perfectly poised to sink into the oblivion of the very center of the earth.

"Well, get on the pumps you DO have and get on them NOW!" he shouted back. On the ship's telegraph, the Captain's last call stood as "all stop," and while he pondered his next move, the anxious, shouting crew, who were wrestling fire hoses in a hopeless attempt to pump the overwhelming volume of water out of the cargo hold, suddenly made up his mind for him.

"Jesus Christ! Abandon ship! Abandon Ship!"

Sinking fast, the center of the ship was hammering on the outcropping, and the bow's nose started to sag straight down towards the void. Full blown panic rose in the heart of every man on board, all of them soaked to the skin from the rain and the geysers that were shooting out from pumps and hoses everywhere across the ship. They dropped their work where they stood and the abandoned hoses wiggled and sprayed indiscriminately, as men crowded onto the high stern and hastily prepared for rescue. When help pulled alongside, frightened, flailing sailors grabbed ropes and swung wildly toward the rescue vessel, leaving all their personal belongings behind. A few of the Kirk Pride's men missed the rescue ship completely on their first pass on the rope and banged into its side, nearly slipping into the sea. Fortunately, all but one of the men aboard knew how to swim and the lone non-swimmer, a Jamaican cook, had long since donned the only life saving device he could find; an oversized, battered, life ring that squeezed him tightly around the middle. Too scared to move, he grabbed onto the rescue line with a grip so fierce, and a consciousness so single minded, that no one could get him to let go of the rope. The rescuers tried begging, cajoling and cursing him, but his grip only got tighter. He was paralyzed with fear. Eventually, someone had to pry his fingers away from the rope with so much force that the crackle of breaking bone could be heard above the commotion.

By the time it was over, the 177-foot ship lay split and wounded, bleeding her crew, totally aground on the razor's edge of the rocks in George Town Harbor. No one could believe it had happened.

Back on land, at about 4:30 PM, Bob Soto's phone rang with

a call from the unhappy owner of The Kirk Pride. Soto was quite a celebrity throughout the Cayman Islands because he was the kind of golden, intrepid man that other men dream of being. He was the very first diving operator in the Cayman Islands, or anywhere in the Caribbean for that matter, opening Bob Soto's Diving Ltd. in 1957. It might have been Columbus who discovered some "rocks" covered with tortoises at Cayman Brac, and he only found that much after he'd been blown off course, but it was Bob Soto who really introduced the riches of these islands to the rest of the world. Using some diving equipment he had constructed at home in his workshop, and actually trusting this rickety paraphernalia to work, he set out to dive the local reefs and one plunge was all it took. Bob fell so deeply in love with the kaleidoscopic world he found, that he started soliciting the few tourists who were around to come and share the adventure with him. He only charged a, Cayman Dollar, or two, to rent the equipment, and sightseers lined up quickly. Before Bob, scuba diving was the exclusive territory of scientists and lunatics. No one ever dove for recreation before he set up shop. It didn't take long for the sport to become the national pastime. Today, the diving industry was the number-one tourist draw of the entire region, and for that, everyone from Key West to Jamaica owed a debt of thanks to Bob's folksy charm.

The owners of The Kirk Pride wanted to ask Bob if he could bring his small boat, suitably named "whatever Bob named his boat", out into the storm and pull on the stranded ship hopeful that, however broken the big craft might have been, there was still a chance it could come home afloat. Bob already knew that on an island as small as this one, he had to lend a hand to his neighbors when they needed it or, one day, he might find himself as high and dry as the freighter he was being summoned to rescue. His wife Suzy had to answer the phone when the shipping company called because Bob was already on his way.

Pulling "whatever Bob named his boat" out of her shelter, he hooked up some Hawser lines and, with only 40 feet of boat, headed out into the storm to haul 177 feet of sinking ship back home. When he arrived at the wreck, he was disheartened by what he saw. The Kirk Pride was hooked tightly on the rocks and there were holes in her everywhere. Still, he felt that with a little ingenuity, the ship could be salvaged. Remarkably, after 45 minutes of determined and calculated tugging, Bob started to hear the hull scrapping free from the rock, and inch-by inch, he managed to loose the ship from the outcropping. Not many men would have had the patience or skill to do such a thing, but Bob seemed oblivious to the stinging rain and wind and was pleased with how the operation was going. He believed he would have her moved and secured in no time.

As he towed the wounded Kirk Pride out to its new moorage, the ship looked remarkably well for the immense amount of damage it had sustained. Relieved shoreline onlookers even ran to get their cameras to take a snapshot or two of the ship that had almost sunk in their harbor. Bob planned to fasten her offshore at the originally chosen destination by the Pageant Beach Hotel but as soon as he dropped the Kirk's anchor to the sandy floor 60 feet below, the boat groaned painfully, tilted to starboard, and the bow dipped even farther below the surface.

The cabin and the engine room of the Kirk Pride were by this time so swamped with water from the still unnoticed open forward hatches that even a one-eyed man blind drunk on the shore could see that he was witnessing the last moments of a ship that would not be saved. Huge bubbles belched from inside her as water replaced air in all pockets of the vessel and Bob had no intention of letting the sinking hulk drag "Whatever Bob named his boat" down with it. He unhooked his lines and watched for a while as the big ship sank farther and farther below, with the raging storm and the Cayman sunset a perfect backdrop for her demise. At 6:30 PM, he received one final desperate radio call from the owners begging him to don scuba gear and plug as many holes in her as possible before the Kirk Pride was completely submerged. It was getting very dark, the squall was still in full force, and Bob Soto was not a fool. He didn't even know the layout of that ship and one man in scuba gear battling a sea that was as determined to take its victim as this one was absolute lunacy. As politely as any man whose life was being valued below a few hundred tons of scrap metal could do, he told The Kirk Pride Shipping Company where they could stick it.

The next morning, Bob and his son Danny received another, more subdued, phone call from the shipping company asking again if they could dive. This time, the request was to locate what was now being called the wreck of The Kirk Pride. The sky was clear and the sea calm, so it was an entirely different scenario than the night before. Diving was not only Bob's lifeblood, it was also his passion, and a shipwreck was always particularly interesting. He and Danny called their friend, underwater cinematographer Jack Mc Kinney and together, they loaded up their gear and prepared to go as deep as necessary to find the Kirk Pride.

Firing up "Whatever Bob named his boat", they set out to the exact same spot where the ship had gone down. With tanks, dive lights, weights, and film equipment in place, they dropped over the side and dove down to the anchor chain of the missing ship, using it as their starting point.

From the anchor's base, still mockingly secure in the place it was let fall the day before, the chain led in the direction of the drop off and ended in a violently snapped link. Continuing that direction, they found nothing at sixty feet, nothing at 100 feet, and nothing even at 250 feet. They went so deep in fact, that Bob's Rolex dive watch and his Nikonos camera finally flooded beyond repair, but the ship was gone without a trace. Except for a couple of bits of hatch and deck debris here and there, it was almost as if the 500 ton ship, anchored here only yesterday, had never existed at all. Common sense told Bob that the strong underwater currents from the storm had probably moved the ship away from shore and over the Cayman Wall into the trench but, without any visual clues, there was just no telling what had happened to it. Diving much farther than 250 feet simply wasn't done in those days before mixed gasses and there were no sub operators running at the time. It looked as if Soto was out another thousand dollars in ruined equipment and the Kirk Pride Shipping Company had lost its main source of income forever.

At least the people of Grand Cayman were satisfied that every crewmember had been accounted for. The official word was that there were no deaths involved in the wreck of the Kirk Pride, but there was an unofficial word that told a very different story. Rumor has it that there may have been a stowaway onboard that stormy January day, a man from Tampa who was a sailor himself. It was said that this man had jumped bail in several States across the American south on charges of non-support, so, to avoid both prosecution and payment of the astronomical sum he owed all of his ex-wives, he stowed away on the forward hold of Kirk Pride in the dead of night. Silent and hidden, with nothing but a flask of fortified wine for sustenance, he sailed with the ship all the way to George Town. When they arrived, he took special care not to disembark until he was certain that all of the crew had gone ashore the night before the wreck. Celebrating the success of his clever escape plan, he got so wickedly smashed at the Blue Parrot that, at dawn, he had no choice but to crawl back into the ship through a forward hatch, find a quiet place, and sleep it off. Apparently the first hatch he opened proved a bit too tricky for him, so he drunkenly staggered to the other hatch, managed to open it, and slithered inside. He was so dead drunk in fact, he was anesthetized, and he never heard a thing, even as the ship hit the rocks or as the terrified crewmen bailed out yelling. He simply fell asleep in the harbor and woke up with the fishes. The only thing anyone knows for certain about this man was that, who ever he was, if he even existed at all, he was now resting in a deep and watery grave with the remains of the Kirk Pride amongst creatures with daggers for teeth that live in the black depths of the Cayman Trench.

Of course, all this meant less than nothing to me in 1976. On that day, I was twenty-one, and living in Huntington Beach, California, interested in nothing more than catching the next big wave or some girl's attention. I had no idea that this shipwreck on the other side of the world was even happening and I certainly had no clue that it would haunt my dreams and shape my work for years to come.

I'd come to Huntington Beach by way of Corpus Christi, Texas, an oil town on the Gulf of Mexico. Marine life always loomed large in my world, not only because my hometown was on the water, but because my father made certain that the unadulterated awe he'd always held for the sea and its creatures was also felt in every bone in my skinny, little-boy body. My Dad was a happy, smiling, loveable man, proud of his Hispanic heritage, and very big into family. When you're young, and you worship your old man the way I did, you pick up that sort of enthusiasm like a human Xerox machine and make it your own. Life in our home was like life for any other family in that company town, with its day-to-day pressures and monotonies, until we went to the beach. On those days, we got to step out of the ordinary, colorless reality of school drudgery, chores, and oil refineries, and into another world: A sparkling world of mercurial changes and limitlessness, where creatures shaped like stars made themselves at home. Those days, my father could hardly contain himself.

"Look, son, "he'd said, "Look at the beach. See this shell? Did you know that the scallop who lived in it had almost a hundred eyes. Isn't that something?" You could feel his joy. He waved a hand toward the sea like he was casting a spell. "And all this water meets the other seas and covers two-thirds of the earth's surface. Did you know that? I was reading the other day that humans have explored less than 1% of the oceans, so the biggest exploration in the world hasn't even been done yet." He squinted out towards the horizon. "God only knows what they'll find out there."

He taught me to surf when I was nine, and by the time I

reached my teens, I was a total longboard junkie. The beach was only about fifteen miles from my house, and nothing stopped me from making that trek every day, sometimes twice a day, to ride the waves. I begged rides. I hitched them. I even walked barefoot through the rocky, roadside dust, with an eight-foot surfboard balanced on my head until some softhearted passing motorist took pity on me and picked me up. I did whatever it took to get out into that other realm, because, thanks to my father, the ocean had become my cathedral. While other guys were out doing the typical teenage stuff, I was at the beach doing dawn patrol and literally living the best part of every day in the ocean. I experienced the hot welts of jellyfish stings, the fever and rash of sea lice, and all the cuts and scrapes you have to endure in the course of engaging the sea, but I could have cared less about trivialities like spilled blood. The ocean was consolation to me. Even in the snow, when I had to pick the ice out of the trunk lock on the family car to get the key in to load my board, I went out to surf.

My Mother, like all mothers since the dawn of time, worried that I had become so obsessed with this one, single pursuit that I wasn't allowing myself the kind of well-rounded experience she wanted for her child. Trust me when I say that Mom, usually a sweet-tempered, gentle woman, could show some real teeth when it came to anything that she felt interfered with her children's best interest. Once, shortly after my family moved into our new house in a previously all-white neighborhood in Corpus Christi, an unfortunate neighbor made the mistake of circulating a petition designed to send the Hispanic family that had been nervy enough to buy there packing. We ignored it for a while, but it got a little harder to overlook when the petitioner had the nerve to stand on our very own doorstep, clipboard clutched tightly to her breast, and in a crisp voice, attempted to discuss the "problem" with us. Mom tolerated her crap for about a nanosecond, then lit into that skinny, little bitch so hard that, when she was through, the old biddy slid off our step as pale as a Klansman soused in Clorox. Suffice it to say that my mother only wanted the best for my sister and me, and sometimes, she worried that surfing just wasn't cutting it in the way of my educational development.

Dad tried to offer some reassurance, pointing out that my obsession with surfing was just like the endless enthusiasm every kid has for doing something he loved. "Human beings have a million ways to express love," he'd said, "and kids seem to know how to do it best."

He was right, of course. Kids that surfed show the purest kind of love. When we're older, we wished we could make time for the joys of doing something physical like surfing or biking, but felt we have to use some excuse like, "it's great exercise" to even begin to justify the amount of time we want to spend on these soul-enhancing, heart-pounding "time wasters." But, when you're a kid, dragging your board around as best you can, and wrangling it out onto the beach before and after school, it's an expression of the innocence that comes with living in the moment. There was no reason, no rationalization, and no explanation to your behavior other than you're doing it because you loved it. When I surfed, the Vietnam War, the bigotry of our ignorant neighbors, or whatever was happening in the outside world, didn't matter a good goddamn to me because I was lost at sea.

I suppose that's why it should have been obvious to anyone, especially me, that I needed to find work that involved the ocean, but as a kid, I never made the connection. I only moved to Huntington Beach right after high school because the surf was better there and because I was tired of being a longhaired misfit in Texas during an era when a single joint could land you prison for 5 to 15. In California, I felt more at ease.

I found a room in a rambling apartment there, already crowded to the rafters with an assortment of kids like me, all either students or surf shop employees, except for one older guy who was a classic beach bum from his sun bleached ponytail right down to his Huaraches. I only knew him as Rock n' Roll Billy and from the moment we met, I understood why surfing had made my Mom so nervous all those years. His lifestyle suited me just fine, however. I loved the excitement of never knowing who or what was going to show up on our doorstep next, like the day two FBI agents in serious blue suits came calling.

Flashing badges and scowling over my shoulder into the apartment as I cautiously opened the door, they told me they were looking for a man named William Allen Seavers who had listed this apartment as his most recent address. I was pretty sure I knew everybody who lived with me and the name Seavers wasn't ringing any bells so, eyes as wide as the Texas sky, I assured them that no one by that name lived here, but I would be glad to call them if I ever heard from the guy. I must have I looked as innocent as I actually was because they didn't stick around long; just thanked me brusquely and left. Now if they'd asked for "Billy" Seavers I'm sure I would have made an "oh yeah" connection and gone into the back room to wake him up. Poor Rock and Roll Billy almost spent the next few years sleeping it off at San Quentin for draft evasion, but luckily, I was the only one in the whole flat who didn't know his real name.

The Huntington Beach apartment may have been a slice of Eden but it didn't last long. In a year or two, reality started pressing down on me, the way it always did on kids teetering on the brink of adulthood. My parents had divorced, so I was determined to do the "right" thing with my own life. I just wasn't exactly sure what the right thing entailed, although in a stunning change of attitude, I was pretty certain I didn't want to end up like Rock and Roll Billy. A medical career seemed like a challenge, and it could give me the sort of respect and ready cash all young men longed for. More to the point, I thought having a doctor in the family might even be enough to heal a few of the emotional wounds we all suffered in the aftermath of the divorce. I got very serious about my studies very quickly, finished my degree on schedule, and was accepted into Med School.

Surfing was all but forgotten by the time I did a clinical clerkship at St. Barnabus, a teaching hospital in the South Bronx that was so rough one of my patients was shot to death with a silencer during the two minutes I left him alone in his room. The strange thing was, when the shooting happened, I didn't feel anything I was supposed to feel like shock or anger or fear. I just passed it off as another gloomy incident in the daily perdition of the real world.

I hated what I was becoming. I found no joy or challenge in my day-to-day routines and I couldn't understand why. Only one year away from receiving my M.D., I quietly realized that I was also about one day away from having an educational breakdown. I wanted out.

The moment my plane left La Guardia, I felt every muscle in my body relax, and some of them hadn't been unclenched for years. I returned to Santa Barbara, bought a sailboat and rediscovered the crystalline joys of living by the sea while I still had lots of future to contemplate. One quiet California evening, a man from the boat in the slip next to mine pointed out that, since I loved the water so much, maybe I should try to find my life's work somewhere in the sea. He told me that true success wasn't about raking in the money nearly as much as it was about finding work you love enough to do for no pay at all. Strange how an old adage like that could still harbor so much truth it incites a personal revolution every day.

I enrolled in a local course of study in Marine Diving Technology at the Marine Institute in Santa Barbara, finished the twenty-four month program in less than a year, and was promptly hired as a pilot for a brand new submersible company in Maui. At last, I was living a life that was authentically, irrevocably, my own.

Maui was magical. The sea life there wasn't just beautiful, it's unusually fearless of humans, and I was introduced to one of its principal ambassadors during an early training dive in Hawaii. I was floating in the sub on calm water, concentrating on my preparations for descent, when a Humpback whale abruptly surfaced, right at the nose of my ship, rocking it wildly and nearly giving me a heart attack. According to Hawaiian law, you aren't allowed to run a sub in the presence of a whale because it could possibly frighten the animal and interfere with its migratory progress, so as soon as I stopped trembling and could form a thought, I shut off the engine and sat there, bobbing in the water, eye-to-eye and six feet away from a giant smiling whale. It was a moment too breathtaking to last. I imagined that once the whale got a really good look at my co-pilot and me, she'd figure out we weren't Humpbacks and turn tail and run. But she didn't. She kept circling, fascinated by the two funny looking mollusks in the ugly floating shell. I wasn't sure what to do, so being the creative thinker I am, I put my hand up and waved hello. Astonishingly, the whale lolled onto her side, passed us waggling a fin, and waved back.

For the next several minutes, I flapped my arms and hands like a kid playing shadow puppets on a wall and my co-pilot and I watched incredulously as a 60,000-pound animal rolled around in the water and mimicked my moves with her flippers and fluke. If I needed any more confirmation that the sea was where I belonged, I had it now. There was no doubt I had found my place in the world.

So when the chance to work in the Cayman Islands came up, I was all over it. At 26,000 feet deep, the Cayman Trench might just as well be bottomless, and I was given unlimited access to two research submersibles, toys worth a million and a quarter a piece, to go anywhere I liked it as long as I stayed safe and came back in one piece. The job also came with lodging at Sunset House, a famous diver's hotel on the water in George Town, and a maid named Mavis who had a gorgeous grin like a Jamaican devil and a penchant for voodoo. Add to that the countless shipwrecks littering the seas around me, and I was in Heaven. Even if there was a rusty sign right outside my door that pointed to a nearby outpost called "Hell"

I did have some concerns about sharing housing with my new co-workers at first, but once I met them, my doubts faded away. My roommates were Dave, a boyish looking sub pilot with a well-spoken way about him, who had logged about the same number of dives as me, and Steve, a great big guy who had once tried out with the LA Rams. Steve didn't have quite as much deep time under his belt as Dave and I did, so over our first few weeks in the Cayman Islands, we started to call him "Biff" because whenever something went wrong with a dive, Steve was usually at the helm. As large as Biff was, he could be a bit delicate at times, crinkling his nose and objecting to the smell of what I was cooking, or whipping out some God-awful aerosol spray that actually made the bathroom smell worse than whatever it was he was trying to cover up. In spite of these quirks though, we got along famously, and our favorite gathering place was the kitchen table of our |small apartment.

One evening, I came out of my room to find Dave and Biff just coming home from a dive, looking pale and upset. They both seemed a little too eager to break into a cold beer.

"Bad Day?" I asked holding out my hand for a drink.

"You could say that," said Dave, putting an open bottle into my hand as he passed. Steve still had his head in the refrigerator.

"What happened?" I said, taking a swig and looking back and forth at them. Dave went to sit at the table while Steve busied himself with a sandwich, not looking at either of us. I pulled up a chair next to Dave who started to tell the story.

"Well, we had a biologist on the sub today and she was a little bit, how do I put this, large. Okay. She was a lot large."

"Yeah?" I said, trying to picture how large.

"Yeah, and when she was getting into the sub, she had a really hard time getting past Steve, and I guess her boobs smashed right into Steve's face and that sort of started the whole ball rolling."

"That's large, "I said, nodding.

Steve spoke. His voice was barely audible. "I couldn't breathe for a minute, but it wasn't her fault." Dave looked back at me and continued.

"The dive went okay, but when they came back up, Biff didn't want to go through the whole suffocation routine again, so he tried to give the lady room to get out of the sub first. She got around him and was on the ladder trying to climb out of the sub, but she got stuck halfway out. I'm talkin' stuck. Right in the hatch, sealed in there tight."

I swallowed a mouthful of beer in surprise. "You're kidding me," I said.

"Wish I was, "said Dave. "I was on top pulling on her and Biff was on the bottom pushing on her and that poor lady was just crammed in there like you wouldn't believe."

"There was no air," said Biff solemnly. "It was bad." He took a long draught off his bottle.

"So after fifteen minutes of giving instructions to the woman," said Dave, "and no one being able to budge her an inch, she started to sweat and that started to smell and Biff was taking the brunt of it with no ventilation down below her so he panics and starts pushing on her butt to get her out. Every time he pushes, though, the lady farts. She must have farted right in his face twenty times."

I slapped my hand to my forehead in disbelief and started laughing.

"He's down there pushing, and she's farting and they're both sweating and it gets so ripe that Biff can't take it anymore and blows chunks all over the bottom of the sub."

"It really stank then," said Steve staring straight ahead as somber as a coroner. I started howling with the kind of laughter you're sure you're going to die from for lack of air.

"So we had to call for back up and the Mother ship was dispatched," said Dave, waving his bottle around for emphasis, "And we all put our heads together and we came up with the idea of using Dow silicone grease to rub around her middle. "He shook his head. "That poor lady lost all her dignity and a whole of lot skin."

The woman finally made it out and the only other injury that came out of the whole incident was when I hit my head on the floor falling off my chair laughing. From that moment on I knew life on the surface with these guys would be almost as interesting as life on the sub.

The very next morning, I had an appointment to take a Canadian engineer and his wife down on an adventure tour to see the wreck of the Kirk Pride. I set my alarm early to give me plenty of time to be up and raring to go, and even though

I had to force myself to roll out of bed in stages when it rang, I could feel the first curl of a sleepy smile pulling at my lips right before I opened my eyes. It was great to wake up to a job I loved. In the few short months I'd been here, I'd done hundreds of dives and had already memorized every detail of the Kirk Pride, from the faded lettering on the stern to the broken railings on the bow, but I couldn't wait to get on the sub and go down again. This was going to be just another day in paradise.

The bathroom mirror told the story of the spontaneous party the night before in a couple of noticeably dark circles under my eyes. A clear-headed operator is crucial to every dive, so I decided to really take my time getting ready that morning. I had a big breakfast and a cool shower, and because the dive wasn't going to be a long one, I even indulged in a usually forbidden half cup of strong coffee. When we go down on long dives, I have to cut my fluids off at midnight. There are no bathroom facilities on a little sub like PC1203, only zip lock bag "mission extenders" that are clumsy to use and unpleasant to store. I shaved closely, put on a crisp, white uniform, and on the boat ride out to the launching platform, I tilted my head upwards and felt the rush of marine air in my face. By the time I arrived at the sub, I was clear as crystal and ready to take on anything the deep could throw my way. It was a good thing too, because as I shook hands and introduced myself to the Canadian couple, I didn't have a clue that this dive was going to rock my world.

These days, no one dives The Kirk Pride anymore because of the danger. It's not that the dive itself is particularly perilous, although an 800 foot depth is nothing to sneeze at, but because the area directly above it has become an anchorage for giant modern cruise ships. Along with everything thing else in the Cayman Islands, the Cruise Ship Industry has grown exponentially, and more Princess and Royal Caribbean Luxury Liners crowding into George Town Harbor means finding more places to put them. Unfortunately, one of the more ideal locations to anchor a huge ship was directly above the spot where the Kirk Pride teetered on a ledge below. If I were to take passengers down to the wreck today, and any sort of emergency required me to surface, it would be disaster, like surfacing with a ceiling above. Once starting up from a certain depth, it's exactly the same as pressing a buoy down underwater then letting it go. There is just no way to stop it from rocketing to the surface. This day though, there wasn't a big ship in sight, and my little yellow Perry Class Submersible had the run of the deep.

The Canadians made themselves comfortable in the small space next to the big view port while I did the safety checks and settled in above them in the tower. Biff did a final walk around, I closed the hatch, and we were lowered into the water by our mother ship, Igor.

PC 1203 had always been my favorite. It's one of a pair of three-man submarines that were originally used in the 1980's to seek out oil on the floor of the icy North Sea. A creative light bulb must have gone off in some marketing genius's head after seeing them, because in 1985, they were abruptly purchased and shipped down to the Cayman Islands, about as far away from the world of snow and ice as you can get. There, they were reborn as the only vessels available on this planet that could take ordinary tourists on a dive 1200 feet below the surface. Up until then, that type of adventure was only reserved for people like daredevil oceanographers or National Geographic camera crews, but today any Cayman tourist who wanted to go farther down the wall than a pair of swim fins could take them, and who was rich enough to lay down the kind of cash this "look-see" would cost them, was chauffeured into the abyss, in practically temperature-controlled luxury.

For the true deep freak, the sturdy little PCs offered the ultimate thrill ride, and I enjoyed taking a pair of wide-eyed day trippers down to 1000 feet, blowing their minds with the sights, and getting them safely home again. It's exactly like taking people for a quick joyride into outer space. The only difference was that we headed south instead of north on take-off, and that more people had actually been in outer space than had ever seen the sights below 1000 feet.

"PC 1203, you are clear to vent and dive."

The Canadian couple seemed to be in high spirits right after I closed the hatch, but their happy chatter stopped the instant they heard the whirring of the motor and the heave of water filling the ballast tanks that started our descent. Passengers always got quiet at that moment. Adam's apples gulp with apprehension when we finally became immersed and passengers watched the waterline pass away from the view port. The small, steamy, quarters of the sub seemed even more cramped with the deep blue of the Caribbean pressing down on them, and the reality of going to such a dangerous depth with nothing but a pane of glass standing between their little bench seat and certain death started to sink in. Everyone gets very solemn and very silent for a second; but it was only for a second. At a mere thirty feet below, the kaleidoscope of coral along the Cayman Wall made passengers gasp for an entirely different reason. They were awed.

Forgetting the danger completely, the Canadians pressed their noses up against the view port, and the questions started flying.

"Is that the coral reef?"

"Is it alive?"

"How many different kinds are out there?"

"How deep are we?"

"How far down are we going?"

Tour guide was part of my job description, so I started by explaining that The Cayman Islands were not really Islands at all, but the tips of three undersea mountains 5 miles high. The second tallest mountain in the world, K2, stood just a bit higher than the trench was deep, so this dive was going to be sort of like climbing the Himalayas in reverse.

I pointed to a yellow seahorse playing around a purple sea fan and told them, "The coral and its relatives like that sea fan really are living, breathing creatures, and they only form reefs like this in tropical waters at a shallow depth. Conditions are perfect for them here though, so there are about 100 species that call this place home."

The engineer stared intently out the view port, particularly fascinated by the aptly named brain coral. He leaned closer to get a better look at its perfect parabola and all its little "neural" groves, then sat back and nodded as if he finally understood something. "So that's what happened to my ex-wife's brain," he muttered to himself.

I raised an eyebrow and started to wonder who I was going down with.

Piloting a Perry Class Submersible was a lot like driving a remote control car, if the driver were actually sitting in the car's tiny driver's seat and looking out through a funhouse windshield, that is. On a crowded sub like this, the pilot sat just behind and above the passengers with his head scarcely surrounded by a tower that gave him a 360-degree view of the space around him. I was lucky to work where I did because the water around the Cayman Islands had an unusually high visibility of nearly 200 feet. There were no rivers or streams cutting through the limestone Islands and therefore, no run-off to fill the ocean with silt. But all water, even clear water, had a refractive property that was enhanced by the concave glass we use to see through it. As my passengers looked out the big round view port in the front of the sub at the sponge belt, for example, they thought that they were close enough to actually reach out and touch one of the sponges but in truth, we were a full 65 feet away from the face of the wall. Every fledgling submariner had to learn the hard way how to properly judge distances underwater. Ask Biff.

A lot of people still carried around a "Voyage to the Bottom of the Sea" image of a submarine pilot in their heads. They pictured a perspiring naval officer sitting in front of a huge control panel covered with blinking lights and sonar screens, scowling in concentration while he twisted a baffling array of switches and dials with the fate of the Western world in his capable hands. Although that image made me look cool as hell, the truth was, I operated my sub with a little black box, about nine inches square that held a series of joy sticks and sat quite comfortably in the middle of my lap.

Piloting a sub, like everything else in life, came with practice, and over the years, I've learned to manipulate these controls so easily with one hand that I could literally make that little PC1203 dance.

The engineer spoke up from below. "I was expecting some sort of pressure in my ears, but I don't get that sensation at all on this sub."

"Nah," I replied, "It's completely pressurized in here. But in a moment, you will feel a change in the temperature. The deeper we go, the less sunlight there is so the temperature in the sub drops just like that," I snapped my fingers. "You can really feel it."

And right on cue, the temperature started to fall and the water began to change in color from aqua to an intense blue. Up in the coral reef, which flourishes between 0 and 200 feet, you could still see dapples of sunlight as it drifted across the wall, playing up the coral's ornate patterns and setting the silver and gold hues of the bright little fish that darted in and out among them on fire. But by the time you arrived at the sponge belt, between 200-600 feet, there was much less sunlight and the water became a deeper and deeper shade of midnight until it finally faded to black. Sponges thrived in this darker world because they were not as dependent on the sunlight as corals were. What's more, competition for the sponge's favorite treat, sea snow, a tasty mixture of tiny corpses and feces, was practically non-existent that far down.

All around the world, in every ocean, there was a constant storm of sea snow, and it was no exaggeration to say that this decaying material was probably the basis for all life on the planet. It fed countless creatures from plankton to the whales that eat those plankton. There was so much of it, it could actually become overwhelming if it weren't for animals like the sponge who were crazy for the stuff. Working like living swimming pool filters, one cubic inch of sponge would consume enough sea snow to leave 30 gallons of seawater per day sparkling clean. Proof that even the lowly sponge had the power to save the world.

It was too dark to see much with the naked eye, so I snapped on my spotlight and trained it on the wall's theatrical display of sponges. There, piled layers deep in every hue, size and shape possible, lay a lush, painted garden of creatures, and the passenger's amazement was palpable. Over 10,000 varieties of sponge lived on this layer of the wall.

Including an iridescent orange Elephant Ear Sponge, a deep violet variety of Tube Sponge, and Rope Sponges in blue, pink, and screaming yellow. Hanging in chains, waving like lacy fans, growing like antlers, or fluttering out in slender stands on the undersea breeze, the Cayman Sponge Belt put on a display that would have made Walt Disney hang his head in shame. There was simply no other place like it, and I could tell by the "ahhhs" of the Canadians that, for this view alone, they were glad they came.

We stayed for a while, silently filling our eyes and hearts with the splendor of the sponge belt, then grudgingly, I turned off the lights and backed away, slowly dropping even further down the Wall to a place where the landscape changed dramatically, and in the blink of an eye. At 600 feet, the haystacks began, and the Canadians commented that it looked as if we had suddenly left the earth and landed on the moon. It did indeed. Without a light, I could barely see the back of my hand since all the white sunlight had already been absorbed layer by layer, first red, then orange, yellow, and green, until everything appeared to be a shade of blue or black. No plant species could endure this eternal night. Even microscopic plants require sunlight for photosynthesis, and the animals that did call this place home were specialized individuals, with evolutionary assets that made them able to circumvent the problems associated with constant darkness. To find them though, divers had to know where to look, and a quick scan of the barren rocky floors revealed nothing but a dusting of gray silt and a lone limestone pillar.

I zeroed in on the limestone. There were tons of these mineral outcroppings in this area, some as tall as 100 feet, named "haystacks" by some diving Midwesterner with a penchant for bad metaphors because they reminded him of the haystacks on his childhood farm in Kansas. To me, they've always looked much more like tombstones than haystacks and whenever I hear that story, and picture the desolation and the strange ambiance of the place, I always thought, "I'm pretty sure we're not in Kansas anymore." I make it a point to cruise around one or two of these pillars every time I was down here though, so I could find some of the critters who loved to congregate around them. Basket stars, porcelain corals, and deep sea gorgonians all loved to use the haystacks for shelter and camouflage, and there were usually tracks in the sand that showed me exactly where to look for more mobile creatures as well. It didn't take me long to find something to show the

Canadians. We lingered for a moment to look at a Serpent Star and when I turned my flashlight beam on it, he raised one of his long, slender appendages and waved me away in a very slow motion dismissal. Lit that way against the dark rock, he looked exactly like a tiny, multi-legged thunderbolt.

In the inky blackness that surrounded us at that depth, there were hundreds of little flashes shooting out here and there in the distance, twinkling like undersea starlight. Bioluminescent organisms, ranging in size from microscopic organisms to the rarely seen 15 foot long Megamouth shark, produced this constant and random sparkling as a chemical reaction designed to fulfill one of three specific functions: A creature lit up because he either wanted to frighten creatures away, lure them closer to mate with, or flash in their eyes and blind them, so they'd be long gone before they even realized they were swallowed. The world down this far was a strange and uncertain place. The rules of survival in the deep sea were that there were no rules. Nothing was sacred or sure when you lived on the edge of a black, gaping, hole that fell into the very middle of the earth. Whenever I was at 500 feet, I felt like I was on the threshold of an entirely different dimension, a place where everything around me was nameless and unfamiliar, and where the laws of reality as I knew them, no longer applied. Maybe that's why they called this place the twilight zone. A lantern fish who lived down here and knew his way around the block for example, might see a bioluminescent flash from the corner of his fishy eye, and race toward it without thinking, all engorged and excited, expecting a quickie with some cute girl of his species, but instead, was speared by the quick fangs of a cleverly lit viper-fish. There's a reason they're called viperfish. Their needle-like lower teeth were so long they jut upwards to well over the top of their heads. No matter who were down there, a plankton, a lantern fish, or even a man in a little yellow sub, no one could ever tell what's coming at them in the abyss.

We were hovering at about 600 feet, when I told the Canadians, "Look down from the view port."

There, a couple hundred feet below us in its shadowy grave, lay the deck of the Kirk Pride. It was such a clear, sunny day on the surface, that there was still just enough incandescence reaching down this far to outline the freighter's eerie gray silhouette. It was a remarkable looking, haunted house of a ship, with rusticles dripping off of every surface. Rusticles were a kind of iron icicle created when bacteria and fungi worked together to consume the metal of a shipwreck. Images of them hanging off the sunken Titanic were everywhere when that wreck was first discovered, and we now knew that these microorganisms could consume a ship at a much greater rate than anyone ever thought possible. In less than 500 years, all that will be left of the magnificent Titanic will be a flat mound of reddish-brown microbial ooze at the bottom of the North Atlantic. Looking down at the Kirk Pride, with its peculiar dripstone hanging off every railing, it looked exactly like a creepy toy boat from an Adams Family play set. I explained to the Canadians that, even though the ship seemed tiny in the distance, the "toy" was actually a vessel almost 200 feet length.

I began my approach from the stern, gliding down on a curve to steer clear of the peaks of haystacks along the way. As we got close enough to make out the lettering of the name on the bow, the ship grew larger and the chaos of her last hours

came sharply into focus. Still hung on a rock these many years later, the Kirk Pride leaned recklessly towards the downhill slope, her basic shape intact but looking every inch the Hollywood ideal of a sinister shipwreck. Tangled ropes, and twisted railings were everywhere, some of them hanging off her sides like curled, useless limbs, the result of how the ship fell, end over end, crashing into ledges and bouncing off the wall on the way to it's final resting place. Stalactites and sponges dripped off every surface, but it's nothing like the colorful display of sea life you would find in shallower Cayman shipwrecks like the gorgeous reef in the wreck of the Carrie Lee off George Town. There were no sweet, little fish or flowering corals here. The only coral you would find on the Kirk Pride were rare, deep water species, like the dandelion coral, which looks remarkably like the seed-skeleton of its namesake, except that the lacy tops of this dandelion didn't blow away lazily on the current; They reached out with tiny, stinging fists and snatched and poisoned every zooplankton that happened by. It's a cheerless, somber place; A place that called to mind gothic music and Edgar Allen Poe, dusted in monochromatic deposits of gray ash left by a Benthic storm. If the wreck of the Kirk Pride was not someone's crypt, it surely ought to be.

The Canadians asked me how the ship went down, and since the atmosphere was already spooky, I couldn't resist hamming it up a bit for maximum effect. If it were summer camp, I would have pulled out my flashlight and lit my face from below.

"That freighter didn't stand a chance. The forward hatches were left open and water just streamed into the cargo hold. Men were running around, abandoning ship, leaving everything they owned behind. Everyone got off safely, so they say, but to this day, no one knows for sure how or why those hatches were left open."

We cruised over the aft cargo hold, and an automobile of some unknown model, dusted with sediment and looking like a cold, cement sculpture of the car it once was, stood indifferently on its headlights. On the crushed bridge, the ship's telegraph was frozen in the all-stop position.

"All stop," read the engineer squinting to make out the words. "Man, he wasn't kidding."

The most dramatic feature of the Kirk Pride though, was the way the wreck was perched very precariously on its small stone ledge. Her starboard side hung low, ready to fall off the mountainside at any moment, and since Cayman sat on a fault, it's only a matter of time until an earthquake sends her tumbling down again, maybe this time all the way into the black void of the Cayman Trench.

I returned to the ship's stern and leveled the sub off about 20 feet away so the Canadians could get a good, full view of it, then tilted my head in confusion. Something about this wreck looked wrong to me. Maybe it was the fact that I had just been creating a mood for my passengers, or maybe, as I pilot, I'd been trained to effectively see when something was happening in the dark, but whatever the reason, I could tell that something was subtly and disturbingly strange about this scene today.

Then I saw it. There, on the starboard side of the ship, a rolling light flashed on. It wasn't a light from our sub because all our lights were off, and it wasn't like a bioluminescent fish or any other living light I'd ever seen. It was a lurid glow coming off an object that bobbed in the water, suspended just above the downward leaning deck of the Kirk Pride. The object was cylindrical, about three feet long and a foot in diameter, fully transparent. Inside it was a pure, green light of cool radiance that undulated, like a wave of gooey Luminol inside a test tube. And it was brilliant. It lit up the whole side of the ship.

The Canadians saw it at the same time I did.

"What in holy hell is that?" Asked the engineer.

As if I knew. My jaw was as open as the Kirk Pride's forward hatch. "I, I don't know," was all I could manage to say.

What ever it was, it didn't appear to be afraid of us, and except for the constant undulating, it didn't appear to be moving anywhere either. It just stayed in one, fixed spot, heaving and getting a bead on us, as if it was planning to pass us or zoom out to meet us on course. I was absolutely mesmerized, and I didn't even realize what I was doing with my hands, but I started guiding the sub right into it, getting closer and closer, trying with all my senses to figure out what in God's name I was looking at. When we got as close as three feet away from it, the attention of everyone aboard was so completely riveted on this entity, we could actually hear the beads of condensation inside the sub grow heavy and drop to the floor. None of us could speak because no one had the vocabulary to name or understand or even comment on a moment like this. We just sat there, too stunned to breathe, staring into the green, translucent phosphorescence until I couldn't take it a moment longer. I had to turn on the lights and get a better look at the thing, so I snapped on the switch and cast the sub's elucidating beam into the darkness to reveal, nothing. Absolutely nothing. As unexpectedly as the object came, it disappeared, leaving only a swirl of sea snow behind. Whatever we had been staring at for so hard and so long that our eyes were watering, it vanished in a split second.

The crewmembers gasped as if I'd just done a magic trick, but they couldn't have been anywhere near as astounded as I was.

"What did you do? Were did that thing go?" asked the engineer's wife. She looked left and right out of the view port. "Did the light make it disappear?"

I couldn't say. If it had been something gelatinous I should have been able to make out its form in the light, but plainly there was nothing in front of us. It was impossible for any-thing to be reflecting light on the downward facing side of the ship that way because, except for us, all that lay around the wreck was purgatory and darkness. And anyway, there just isn't any light to reflect at that depth except the light of bioluminescence. One thing I was sure of, we'd just seen an actual object, as real and material as any of us, and not a reflection or a specter of any kind. I snapped off the light to see if I could bring it back, but the thing was long gone. Whatever we had just witnessed, we all knew it was extraordinary, and no one wanted to be the first to talk about it.

After a long, awkward silence, I finally asked, "You guys did see it, didn't you?" I wanted to be sure. When a shocking moment has passed, you almost always had to ask an obvious question to validate the experience and make certain you're not crazy.

They understood and nodded mechanically. "Yeah, we saw it," they both said in unison and then fell silent again. Suddenly, the female passenger's face frowned with concern and her consciousness returned to the here and now. She sniffed the air and asked, "Do you smell smoke?"

Without a doubt, that was the very last question I wanted to be asked when I am 800 feet down in a submarine, but with one quick inhale, I knew she was right. I could smell smoke, acrid, electrical, and strong. The Canadians eyes involuntarily looked towards the overhead hatch as if they were planning an escape through there.

"Hang on," I said, "I'm sure we're okay, but I have to go through a detailed emergency procedure because we're running pure oxygen in here."

I shut off my main systems and blew my emergency air tanks so we could start to rise. Grabbing the flashlight, I looked behind me for any possible source of the smoke. I thought it might be the scrubber, so I took the scrubber apart and smelled the wires. I couldn't really get a handle on it there. Next, I crawled out of the tower and into the machinery space, which was way back in the cone of the sub and shined my light on every modest detail of the workings in there but still no luck. The smell didn't seem to be coming from anywhere, but it was definitely in the cabin and getting stronger by the minute.

I settled back into the tower, and calmly assured the Canadians that all the systems were fine, but we were going to go ahead and surface anyway just to err on the side of caution. Not surprisingly, neither of them put up much of a fight.

I might have been the picture of professionalism on the outside, but inside, I was sweating bullets. This was a submariner's nightmare. The smell of smoke was getting so strong it almost made me gag, but oddly, there wasn't a wisp of actual smoke anywhere in the cabin; just that wretched smell. I started the 24-volt emergency system so I could get a UWT Communication with Biff and let him know we were headed up.

"Atlantis Tender. Atlantis Tender. This is PC 3 at seven five oh feet." My voice was smooth and even. "We have a bit of a problem here. There's a strong smoke smell in the cabin and I can't figure out where it's coming from so we're leaving the Kirk Pride and heading your way."

"Roger that," said the surface, "We'll be ready for you. Keep us informed of any change in your situation." That was the last sound heard in the cabin for the duration of the long ascent to safety.

When we got to the surface, the Canadians rocketed out of that sub like a pair of greased weasels. There were support vessels all around the dock ready to assist us and a couple of engineers immediately crowded past me into 1203, poking here and there, keen to find what was wrong with the sub. There's only room for three at a time in the sub's cabin and since I'd already been over the engine, I decided to let everyone else get in for now while I helped the Canadians onto the boat that would take them back to the harbor.

It was good to feel the hot Caribbean sun again, and the three of us didn't say much as we walked toward the boat. I was holding out my hand to the woman to steady her onto the launch when Dave came walking towards us shaking his head. "Man, are you sure it was smoke you smelled?" he asked, "We can't find a thing that's hot in that whole sub."

The engineer was immediately indignant. "Well, look again," he said, jabbing a finger toward the sub. "Because there was smoke in that thing and it was strong. We smelled it and looked everywhere and we couldn't find it. I've been an |engineer in a power plant for seventeen years and I know smoke when I smell it. I'm tellin' ya . . . It was there." His wife nodded in firm agreement.

I had always been grateful that the man on board with me that day was an engineer and not just another tourist in a Stingray Beer T Shirt and a ball cap. If he had been, everyone might have thought I was just plain nuts. And if they knew that the smoke was only half the story, that I'd also seen a glowing green light, no telling how many people would have lined up to sign the commitment papers.

The search for the smoke continued for a while, so the Canadians and I sat on the boat, waiting and watching while the waves lapped the sides, each lost in our own thoughts. All the others were crawling in and out of the sub like ants on an anthill, deadly serious about uncovering the source of problem. Eventually, one of the technicians, a big Puerto Rican named Hugo, came over and stood by the launch. I watched his huge size 13 shoes approach us on the dock and stop next to me. I thought he was going to talk to us but instead he stood mutely alongside and I could feel his eyes staring down at me. I raised my head and caught him in the act, although he wasn't really looking at any one of us in particular, just vacantly staring at us all with an intense, piercing look. I took a quick visual inventory of both the engineer and his wife to see if they were doing anything that would warrant being stared at that way, but they weren't and Hugo kept right on looking a hole through us. It was starting to make me uncomfortable so I put up my hands in helpless exasperation and asked him, "What? What are you staring at?"

Hugo startled, then rubbed the back of his neck with embarrassment.

"I'm sorry," he said quietly, "I was just thinking that the three of you guys look like you've seen a ghost."

The Canadians and I looked at each other. Then, bursted out laughing.

"Wow," said the Engineer with a wry smile, "Are we that

transparent?" The engineer's wife could hardly contain herself then, and it was at least thirty seconds before her giggles wound down to a little snort of a finale followed by a trailing sigh. She wiped her eyes. Hugo's neck drew back in surprise. Either he wasn't in on the joke, or maybe that smoke in the cabin did have some explanation, after all. It was a pretty weird response for three people who'd just had the bejeezus scared out of them, so he turned and walked over to the sub, whispered something to Dave, then cast a not-so-sneaky glance of concern at us from over his shoulder. Dave smiled and walked back to the launch. His eyes locked on mine and he jerked his thumb towards his chest in a "get out" gesture.

"C'mon, Gary," he said grinning, "Enough with the afterglow. We need you to get back in there and help us figure out what's up with the sub."

It was a fitting choice of words and exactly what I was ready to hear. I immediately shifted mental gears and got out of the launch, impatient to fix my sub, find that damn green light again, and determine for a fact what had just happened to me. I thanked the Canadians with a handshake and they told me they would never forget me, or this dive, as long as they lived, even with therapy.

We spent the next few hours poring over PC 1203, but in the end, every part on her turned out to be virtually factory-new and there was never an explanation for where the smoke had come from. I was working as hard as I could to beat the clock, too, because I really wanted to get back down and see if I could find the glow again, but by the time I was through with system checks it was long after dark and I was too exhausted to go anywhere. I went straight home without pausing to eat and slept a few hours. I got up at dawn. I showered, threw on a T-shirt and shorts and headed out the door with a pattie between my teeth. Thirty minutes later, I was back on the sub and headed down to the Kirk Pride.

Sailing down the wall on my return, I felt a rush of joy wash over me. It's the same familiar contentment I found whenever I was on that crate all by myself. My sub might not have been a shiny, modern vessel with all the latest technical bells and whistles. In fact, it's something of a sad eyed, coughing, jalopy by comparison, but still, PC 1203 was a workhorse, having completed more dives into the mesopelagic zone than any other manned submarine in the world. I'd bonded with it so completely that I knew the meaning of it's every little creak and burp. It's like a living part of me, and when I was sailing in the abyss, I could judge exactly which switch or knob to use by each subtle change in sound, pressure, or current. I piloted that sub by the seat of my pants, and in the world of the twilight zone, it is the sun, moon and stars to me: Its yellow hull acted as a shining armor against the assaults of the deep, it's dependability made it an angel of mercy when things went wrong, and its knack for finding astonishing things few men have ever seen made it a Patron Saint of impossible dreams. Every day down in that sub was a gift, and that day, I was on a mission.

Approaching the wreck again from the stern, I was disappointed to see that the Kirk Pride looked like the same old, dusty, quiet shipwreck it had been for decades. Nothing about it shimmered or moved today except for the occasional frayed end of a rope waving in the current. I decided to hover near it for awhile and just watch, making notes about precisely where I had seen the glow, where it might have come from, and where it may have gone. As much as I loved my work, one of the best-kept secrets about research diving was that for every 100 dives you go on, something really out of the ordinary happened on maybe one or two. The deep didn't give up its secrets easily and coaxing anything from it required not only the proper technology and nerve to go as far down as needed, but also the patience of Job and the ability to sit on your butt until it blistered while you waited for something to emerge. A good pair of eyes didn't hurt either, and as I scanned the wreck, I mentally ticked off items that I knew had always been on the ship.

"Fire hoses. Check. Broken beam. Check."

Nothing seemed out of place so I decided to turn the lights on and get a more detailed look at the specific area where I had seen the glow. I pulled a little closer to the starboard side, turned on the lights, and pointed the yellow beam towards the exact spot where we had come face to face with the ghostly thing. There, on the deck, directly below the spot where the undulating green glow had hovered, lay the pants and shirt of a sailor.

Sea trash, even this far down, was nothing new. Ignorant people everywhere threw all sorts of things into the ocean, and the once pristine waters around the Cayman Islands were no exception. The worst offenders here were usually those who drunkenly ran their boats out to the reefs, crawled all over them, and broke off a bit as a souvenir. You wouldn't believe some of the things that have been pulled from the waters around here. Common things like beer bottles and flip flops of course, but also dead bodies, ancient barrels of rum, and garbage from Cruise Ships. I knew in one beat of my pounding heart though, that these clothes weren't sea trash. They were arranged too smoothly, like they had been on a body that sunk to this deck, then disintegrated. The chambray shirt was laid neatly and directly above the bell-bottom pants as if someone had intentionally set them there, like clothes laid out on a bed for a child. The odds were very long that an evidently matching outfit like this one could have drifted from above and landed exactly that way, in exactly that place, in the last twenty-four hours. Even if you allowed that such a thing could happen, the clothes shouldn't have stayed arranged that perfectly, one atop the other because clothes, soaking wet or not, were lightweight, wispy things that currents could move at will. In the time I'd been watching, they should have fluttered or drifted askew in some way, but they didn't. They stayed exactly as I found them. Flawlessly set, like someone had placed them there deliberately, and there weren't many someones wandering around at 800 foot below the sea. And I knew for a fact the clothes hadn't been there yesterday, because this was the one area of the Kirk Pride I had ogled intensely for several, eternal minutes.

I whispered a flabbergasted, "Wow," and sat back in disbelief.

For a moment, I considered the possibility that someone was playing a joke on me. It would have been just like Biff to rub in what happened yesterday with some stunt like this, but then it occurred to me that I hadn't yet told him, or anyone, about the glowing green light. And besides, at 800 feet, it would be virtually impossible for anyone, least of all Biff, to pull off a practical joke this complicated. Even a technical diver using trimix gasses wouldn't go this far down just to hang out clothes and if he did, he would have had a hell of a time pinning them down that neatly while he worried about his head exploding from the pressure.

Floating alone in the blackness, I remembered all the famously terrifying stories I'd heard my whole life about ghost ships and mermaids and other apparitions from the deep and I couldn't help but wonder; was there something to those tales? Maybe some person really was caught halfway between this world and the next, hovering around this ship where he died and desperately trying to contact someone from the world of the living. If it were true, he certainly picked the perfect means and setting to do it, because here I was, alone in the abyss, imagination running wild and hearing his message coming through loud and clear. Maybe, I thought, there were countless souls trapped in the sea, untold numbers from the Titanic, or the Andrea Doria, or all the boats that had been swept away down the centuries who just wanted it known that they were still here.

I smiled and shook my head. "I shouldn't go there," I said to myself. Still, a new perspective settled down on me that day that had stayed with me ever since. It's just a simple idea, but it had become the single philosophy that drove everything I did; my diving, my study, and even my religious convictions. There had got to be more out there. Whatever we thought we knew about anything, the sea, the heavens, or even the people we love, there was always more than meets the eye. Fact, as we understand it, was in constant flux and I guessed it was just my calling to try and learn as much as possible about this one particular entity we did not understand. The sea held such fascination for me. The 99% of it that my father told me had never been explored has been too much for me to resist. With the eyes of a scientist, and the wonder of a child, I was compelled to rush into it, sharing with the world above every astonishing secret the world below shared with me, until the day I died and maybe my life, too, became a light that would shine in its darkness.

When I got home that night, Mavis was just leaving my apartment, mop and bucket in hand. She stopped on the threshold, took a handkerchief out of the pocket of her blue housedress and wiped the sweat away from her forehead. She looked at me for a long moment as I approached, then grinned a blisteringly white, knowing smile. In her curious Caymanian accent, a wild mixture of Jamaican, Southern, and Scottish lilts, she asked, "See any ghosts down there tonight, Mister Gary?"

I didn't even flinch as I responded.

"Yes, Mavis, I surely did."

I lay in bed that night and started thinking about everything that had happened to me in the last two days, the glow, the mysterious shirt and pants, and Mavis' knowing grin. I'd only been in the Cayman Islands two months and I thought "Is this what I can expect to see from now on? Ghosts and apparitions and voodoo women? What the hell kind of place did I stumble onto?"

I turned off the light and put my head down on the pillow with a grin so wide it hurt. It was just like my dad had said, the sea is a world where anything can happen, and so were the Cayman Islands. Yesterday's dive with the engineer and his wife was only my 300th but I'd already seen so many wonders my head was spinning. So what if I still was a baby pilot? I knew in my soul that I would go on to complete literally thousands of dives and see things no one else had ever seen. It was just like when I was a barefoot surfer in Corpus Christi. I could do this forever and for no other reason than I loved it.

As I drifted off into sleep, the only other reality that was even close to the extraordinary feel of the deep, I tried to imagine what "tomorrow" would bring.

The answer, as it turned out, would be something straight out of a nightmare.

4

The morning had arrived with a festive atmosphere in the harbor of George Town Grand cayman. A beautiful clipper ship sat off shore near the site that we were dive that day, ironically the site was called heartbreak ridge and the irony I would learn was a dark history of the Esmerelda.

The ship was a four masted Barquentine, one of the largest sailing vessels afloat. She carries a crew of 271 sailors and 80 cadets. and is said to be a training ship for the Chilean Navy. Her Length overall was 371 feet with a beam 42 feet and was a few inches shy of 20 foot draft. Her hull was made of steel and she was rigged as a four-masted barquentine and was built in 1952 and calls Valparaiso her home.

Amnesty international had said Esmeralda was used by the Chilean Navy as a center of detention and torture in the port of Valparaíso as early as1973. One hundred and twelve political prisoners and their families were tortured there and eventually disappeared.

The rumor going around the Island was that Cayman authorities were looking to question one of the sailors on charges of sexual assault on one of the local Caymanian girls. And no doubt the Cayman authorities were surprised to see the ships hasty departure into international waters where the accused was tried convicted and sentenced on board. A video tape was sent to the police in Cayman of the accused hung by the neck from the yard arm of the ship.

It was during that hasty retreat I found myself descending down the wall with an ex Navy seal named Dean. We were in a deep conversation about the immensity of the ocean and the minute chance of seeing anything over two or three feet long. You see I said, 97 percent of all the living space on the planet is in the great oceans and seas of the world and the chances of us seeing anything was just so slim. It would be like coming from another planet and landing in the sahara desert and asking were all all the people. The great animals of the ocean are around just not always here.

I did share a story that my roommate dave had told me a few weeks earlier. He was descending the great mountain of grand cayman and having a friendly discussion with an engineer from Cable and wireless. Dave had been assigned to follow a telephone cable that was being laid by a Cable laying ship above. It was laying a three inch cable from Grand Cayman to

Jamaica. The cable laid down the wall to the silty slope without a hitch. But Dave's sixth sense kicked in and he popped his head up the tower and looked aft just in time to witness a giant tail swimming away. He did not recognize the tail and said it was like nothing he had ever seen.

As we approached 500 feet I could see in the distance that there had been an avalanche and silt had formed thick clouds arranged in layers by the ocean current. The clouds of silt were stretched out by the thermal clines that had created currents between the epi and mesopelagic zone.

The low light made the clouds look surreal with the mountain in the distance. As we would go through on layer we could see the flattened underside. "The six hundred foot thermal cline in pretty much found in all the world oceans," I told Dean, "and act as a physical and physiological barrier for many animals above and below the barrier. The salinity and temperature change here are dramatic." What caused the avalanche in the first place? asked Dean. It was the Esmerelda pulling her anchor at the edge of the wall. Pull one big boulder down on the loose sediment in this steep wall and you cause a enormous avalanche.

Once again the visibility was decreasing as we descended deeper. Along with loss of ambient light the clarity of the water was diminished to nothing in some spots. But fortunately it was between layers and at times I could see a haystack I recognized and set my course from there, nevertheless you couldn't predict the thickness and the descent was another white knuckler. As we approached 1000 feet I asked dean if he wanted to check out a cave with me. I briefly told him about the incident had occurred with Jason and myself in the same area. I also had a sounding board for my theory's. I told him I had picked up Richard Ellis's book Giant Squid last time in Miami and read it cover to cover. I determine that Architeuthis was only found in very cold water and his blood would boil in water in the high 50°F. But Ellis did say look in the caves.

Before I finished my thought Dean replied "Hell yeah, let's go!" I turned my ballast valves back in line and free flowed water back in the submersible and headed for the caves at 1150 foot level, the same area we were blinded so tremendously before.

The silt clouds were above us now but descending and would be blinding by the next hour. I followed the haystacks to the sheer face of the mountain that contained the enormous cave. The mood had switched to a more powerless feeling as our hearts were in our throat pounding way above normal with anticipation. I turned on the lights at the cave entrance. I guess my build up was anticlimactic, there were unusual fish with large eyes up on the fenestrated walls of the cave and the floor was covered with hermit crabs all walking in the same direction. I hovered in front of the cave with nothingness below us and tons of water above us, a small speck in front of a giant Everest.

I think we should go in a little and see what's behind the corner, I said. The gave entrance was large but it wedged itself with the ceiling and floor eventually meeting abut 20 feet in. We would only have six inches above when we set down ion the silty bottom. Look, screamed dean, What?

The left turn of the cave we could not see was bellowing silt. It was a thick enormous cloud that engulfed the sub. And for one quick millisecond I saw a large appendage stick to the viewport. It was like nothing I had ever seen.

The Cave filled with sea snow which stayed suspended for what seemed like forever. In our blindness, would the creature return? I thought. I felt confident that nothing would happen to our sub, she was built like a tank. We were not that deep inside the opening of the giant caverness hallow, however, It would be prudent to wait for the silt to settle enough to get a clue where the walls of the cave were before moving. Getting wedged inside a subsea cave nobody new about was first off a slow painful demise because there was no rescue down here for at least a week. A subject Dean and I had discussed on descent.

After several minutes and the gift of an uncommon subsea current we were able to back from the cave and start our ascent. The excitement inside the sub was electric. What was that? We must have said twenty times on the long ascent through the deep mesopelagic zone.

My mind focused on the obvious, I learned an adage in medical school that said, when you hear the sound of hoof beats don't assume there are zebras. I thought maybe a cephalopod, like a squid or an octopus. A giant octopus? maybe. I had seen a very large octopus and filmed him from a distance. He was an epic creature and would probably stretch ten foot from arm tip to arm tip. He would galop like a horse and when he stopped and stood his ground he would stomp his long arms and inflate his head shaking it from side to side as to intimidate us. After a short while he came close enough to judge his sex.

The millisecond splat of an appendage on the viewport was a thick skinned surface and not a tentacle of an octopus which would have been shinny and semi transparent through a 600 watt light. No, I thought the skin color was dense, a dead grey color like a mummy. The surrounding color of the sea snow and or the cave walls is what I would suspect a giant octopus to be. In my gut I new it was not an octopus. the initial bellowing of the sea snow was more violent then our local intelligent octopus could have achieved.

Dean had talked of a diver in California that would scuba dive off his boat far out to sea and hang off a line at 150 feet with large lights and a camera. "I heard something huge come out of the dark," Dean said, "and wrap him up and took away his camera, mask and snorkel , leaving him searching for a backup breathing device." Yes, I had heard many versions of that story and new it had been a Humbolt squid, hardly the culprit on this side of the world, but a squid non the less was a true possibility.

5

On any given day in Mauricio Solis' brief life, he could probably be found freediving somewhere in the warm, cobalt blue waters off Mexico, even those days when it was only in his dreams. A tanned, broad-shouldered young man, Mauricio would arm himself at every opportunity with good bait, a diving buddy, and a very sharp spear gun, and somehow wrangle a ride from his home to the ocean's edge. There, both he and his friend would put on a pair of long, narrow swim blades, a type of swim fin specifically designed for freedivers, and leisurely guide a rented boat out to an area far from shore, one of countless favorite spearfishing spots that had always seemed lucky to him. Calmly, the two young men would discuss their battle plan for the day. There was no question between the boys about who was going to be the shooter and who would be the back-up. Mauricio had been

127

swimming for nearly as long as he'd been walking and his success as a spearfisherman was the talk of his hometown. He was, without a doubt, the logical choice to be the one to go down with the gun.

Freediving is a wickedly dangerous sport, rather like scuba diving, without the equipment. Mauricio was its master. He hopped cheerfully into the water and waited patiently for his friend to pass down his speargun to him. Gaining full control of usually autonomic functions like respiration and heartbeat isn't an easy thing for anyone to do, especially while being tossed around by waves in the sea, but after a moment or two of acute concentration, Mauricio would take three or four deep long cleansing breaths, fill his lungs to bursting with good air and, holding tight to the gun, turn nose-down into the water, slowly fluttering his swim blades all the way down to 60 feet.

Visibility in the water was good and Mauricio could see quite a |distance around him even at that depth. The life in the sea; the jellyfish, the seaweed, and the small fish; told him all he needed to know about the movement of the current. He just trailed his bait out and watched it catch on the under-tow, wiggling as if it were still alive; a perfect undersea cast, and he knew it. Hanging suspended half way between the blue sky and the soft floor of the sea, he checked his dive watch and made note that he had been holding his breath for two minutes now, so his air was still plentiful and fresh. He always started his hunts this way, peering deeply into the blue void of the sea, just waiting and watching.

In an instant, he could feel in his gut that something about his surroundings had changed. A life force of some significant size had caught the scent of his bait, and at the very moment this thought was forming in his head, a shadow abruptly materialized in the distance. Mauricio could not yet see his prey clearly, but very clearly, his prey had seen him. His heart started to beat a little faster, and unconsciously, his finger tightened on the trigger of his gun. The shadow hovered for a moment, then unexpectedly, rushed towards him. In a half-second of revelation, it became comprehensible as a school of scad mackerel, and although there was a moment of disappointment that it was not the Bluefin tuna he was looking for, it was still a promising find. Schools of any mid-sized game fish like mackerel, means tuna will likely come next. The minutes ticked by too quickly however, and his prey failed to materialize. Mauricio's lungs started to burn, and after nearly four minutes, he decided to head up for the surface. Breaking through to the sky, he gasped, and as the air rushed into his desperate lungs, it stung a bit. He took a moment to catch his breath, and sputtered a description of what he has seen to his diving buddy.

"Eso es!" he gasped, wiping water from his mouth, face breaking into a tremendous, white grin with the deep parenthesis of his dimples on either side. "A school of mackerel, so Bluefin should be next, my friend. I'm going to go back down"

Again, three very long breaths, and again, he descended.

He wouldn't go quite as deep this time. The mackerel were hovering at about 30 feet now, so he paused and watched them from behind a stringer of seaweed. His gun was ready to fire, and he floated still, almost motionless, until, just as he had predicted, a hungry Bluefin, a fish the older fishermen called "Blue Devils," finally appeared. It was keeping its distance from both the Mackerel and Mauricio, but he knew his speargun could bridge that distance in a twinkling. He raised the weapon to shoot, gazing down the teakwood stock, skillfully lining up the tip of the pointed barb as his sight, while the tuna circled. Concentrating, Mauricio aimed for the spot just behind the fish's eye in its deep blue upper body. The tuna looked to be almost forty pounds and, once tagged, a fish of such size could easily drag a man to his death.

"Wait for it," he thought to himself. The fish slowed, watching and gathering strength for the rush forward, eager to kill something, anything, and at the exact moment the fish seemed to stop moving, Mauricio pulled the trigger and heard the familiar ripping sound begin. The gun's reel spun so fast it seemed certain to catch fire as the arrow's point flew towards its mark. In silent impact, the spear tore into flesh, and there was a trembling of the great, blue tail. The stunned fish began to fall, and Mauricio swam to the surface to reel it in.

As Mauricio reeled the tuna tight, the fish surprised him, rallying its strength. Mauricio was literally pulled through the water until, luckily, the fish tangled its line on a rock, and became secure enough to allow the boy to head up for air. On the ascent Mauricio realized that all he had to do to complete this catch was hang on tight to his gun, follow the line back, and pith the animal. His head broke free of the surface and he gasped for the air he needed. He didn't have time to talk, but he looked at his friend and winked. Then, he closed his eyes, inhaled deeply and went back down.

He had to work fast. A bleeding tuna was a veritable shark magnet, so, with a heart as full as any warrior's, he swam toward his opponent, grabbed it and stabbed a knife into its fleshy head. The tuna's life flowed out on the current and Mauricio swam back to the surface with the fish still on his line.

"We've got to get this thing in!" he cried to his companion, and the young men let the fish float out on the line as they swam back to the boat. Back at the dock, a crowd of sightseers gathered taking pictures and congratulating them on their good luck. A Bluefin was a rare sight back in the early Eighties, and it's an even rarer one today. Mauricio puffed out his chest at the admiration, and in his face you could see that, however grown-up his accomplishments may have been, he was still a little boy who reveled in the praise of others. Amid all the back slaps and flirting girls, one thing was clear: People were simply drawn to this young man.

As an adult, Mauricio was still blessed with that same charisma. He was a softhearted man, generous to those he loved with both his time and remarkable energy, and the only person I've ever known who enjoyed the respect of practically everyone who ever met him. Considering that the nature of his biggest passion, spearfishing, required that he never dive alone, I guess his likeability was an inspired bit of divine handiwork.

Mauricio was the kind of person you could talk to. It's not so much that he was a big talker himself, but from personal experience I can tell you that he had listening down to a fine art. Whenever it was just he and I alone, whether we were resting between dives, or training on the sub, I found that falling into a conversation with him was as natural as taking a breath. Our conversation was processed in his mind carefully, with a thoughtful look, and a short, to-the-point response that made it clear your message was both heard and understood. I had actually met Mauricio once before he came to George Town, though only briefly, when both he and I were hired to build a sub in Everett, Washington. I recognized him instantly the day he arrived. Through my front window, I watched as he and his fiancée, Susan were getting set up in a room next to mine at Sunset House. I decided I would let them be alone that move-in morning, but on the second day, when I knew he wasn't yet working and I had the day off too, I put on my wet suit and, blades in hand, went over to knock on their door.

When Mauricio answered, he looked at me in surprise. I wasn't sure if he recognized me at first, but as the unspoken message of my diving gear began to register, he damn sure understood what the swim blades meant. His face brightened, and he asked.

"Gary? Are you ready to dive? You're serious?"

I nodded.

The boy from Mexico appeared again in his white grin, and he said, "Wait here long enough for me to grab my stuff!"

We walked cheerfully, but mostly silently, picking our barefoot way across the rocky iron shore to the waters edge. By the time we finally got to the water, we had told a few jokes and swam out to the wall's edge and started doing what guys always do, testing each other a bit. We both wanted to prove how far down we could go, each man trying to outdo the other and, of course, he blew my socks off. I could go to 70 feet, and he could do 100. Not to be bested, I would concentrate, slow my heartbeat as much as I could, and take in so much air that it felt like I could live underwater. I couldn't though. If I did 80 feet, Mauricio did 110. The competition was a little humbling for me, and in short order, I knew I couldn't compete with him as far as freediving went. Luckily, Mauricio was a born teacher who appreciated the fact that I wanted to learn and I was ready to garner everything I could about overcoming corporal limitations from this new, surprising Zen master.

Mauricio and I began diving together on a regular basis. During each of our sessions, he'd encourage me to go a little deeper and stay down a little longer, offering little tricks and tips for fooling my body out of its insatiable need for air. To demonstrate, he would float on the surface, quietly and calmly, staring down at his target depth, letting the surface world drift away from his consciousness and slowing his heartbeat to a mere 40 beats a minute. Then, with a fluid scissor kick, he began to rhythmically paddle down to 60 feet. The whole distance took him no more than 20 seconds because of the aerodynamic efficiency of his swimblades, and I watched him from the relative safety of about twenty-five feet, ready to help him in case something happened during the last fifteen feet of his ascent. That's where most freedivers run into trouble, during the last fifteen feet. Unconsciousness occurs most often at that depth, because the brain was literally starved for oxygen. Fortunately, once a diver had blacked out, he could often be revived. A reaction called the mammalian reflex closed the airways and didn't allow water to fill the lungs. Mauricio always kept his hand on the buckle of his weight belt laboring under the delusion that, should he ever feel himself beginning to pass out, he might be able to release the belt with his last conscious thought and rise to possible rescue.

I watched his hand carefully whenever we dove and took it as a signal of Mauricio's condition. If, in the final few feet of the ascent, he felt okay about his situation, he would take his hand away from the belt and give me an okay sign to let me know that everything was under control, and then I could relax right along with him.

In fact, we developed an entire set of signals like this to ensure our safety; a personal, wordless, supra-conscious vocabulary that required only that I looked at him and be certain he was looking back at me. As I came up, with my hands over my head and my chin to my chest, I raised three fingers in an "okay" sign so he knew I would make it. With a glance he could tell me, "I'm going deep now. I'm going for a 130 foot dive," and I would follow him from the surface. We had to understand each other intuitively because, unless everything was perfect on these dives, there was a very good chance that one of us might pass out. We developed absolute trust, each man holding the other up as surely as the breeze lifted the diving birds that nipped at the water around us.

It was vital to have this kind of trust with a freediving partner, and total lunacy to dive without it. In between dives one afternoon, Mauricio and I were sitting on the edge of the Cayman Wall, literally perched on the edge of eternity, when he told me of another diver we had known in Oahu who had been a victim of Shallow Water Blackout.

"You know," he said, " I used to train with that guy all the time and he was a lot like you, always trying to best his last record. Jeez, he wasn't afraid of trying anything." Mauricio tossed a rock he had picked up off the ledge out onto the water.

"But, he did have this one problem, you know. He never was as careful as he should have been. He passed out on me one time, and I had to hold him up. I barely got him to the surface in time to save his life. I tell you, it scared the living hell out of me." He looked towards the shore, and then back towards me. "Let's always be careful, okay?" he said decisively.

I said, "Yeah, man, let's promise each other we'll always dive together."

He nodded.

And so it was. For the next several months, starting in November we dove the waters that surrounded George Town. There was a kind of paradise period when you got to be really good friends, a time of sheer enjoyment, before you began to discover each other's flaws. It's the best time that guys have together, a time when bonds were formed, and for Mauricio and me, those three months turned out to be that special time. I knew if I had a problem, in or out of the water, that his exact words would be, "Talk to me, Man. I'm your sounding board." And, each day at his doorstep was an adventurous repeat of the day before.

"Are you ready?" he'd ask.

"Yeah, I'm ready."

But Mauricio's love of the deep didn't end at 130 feet. His ultimate ambition was to go as far down into the sea as possible, so whenever we weren't diving in wetsuits and swim blades, we switched our instructor and pupil roles, and I trained Mauricio to be a pilot on the Deep Explorer. In the hushed atmosphere of the cabin at 1000 feet, he and I had a lot of time to chat; to actually talk in a way that physics forbids during a freedive as we explored the areas down the Cayman Wall.

"The sub is gonna fall fifty-five to sixty feet a minute," I told him on our first dive, and he puffed out his lips in derision.

"Man, I can fall that far in less than half that time," he said smiling. "But you gotta open the hatch and let me out."

It was my pleasure to flick a little back at him, "From what I hear, you can fall even faster than that. Wasn't there some girl you had cornered at the Lone Star last night?"

He laughed and looked embarrassed. "No way, Man" he said, shaking his head. "I'm almost a married man."

He'd really light up when he talked about spear fishing though, and the trip he had recently taken to Baja was the crown jewel in a lifelong love of the sport. He had written an article about it that appeared in Skin Diver Hawaii Magazine. But in the Cayman Islands, it was against the law to spear any fish at all, even those that were caught by other means, unless you were lucky enough to be born a local. This was a huge disappointment for Mauricio. Huge. You could see it on his face, as he spoke.

"It's almost enough to make me fake citizenship," he said, sadly. "But I don't think I could fool anybody." He smiled. "I could never get that accent down."

Mauricio told me that on Grand Cayman, in customs, they have a room filled with hundreds of 700 dollar Riffe spearfishing guns, all piled atop one another, squandered and useless, every one of them confiscated from some spearfishing hopeful eager to impale something wild on their trip to the Caribbean. I sincerely felt for those who lost their expensive equipment, but the waters around the Cayman Islands were a marine life sanctuary with good reason. The sea life here might have been breathtaking, but all the corals, fish, and sponges that made up the colors in this kaleidoscope, were completely interdependent. The extraordinary increase in tourism over the last fifty years had forced the local government to take certain steps that would guarantee their protection. One man with a spear gun might have been as natural as a barracuda hunting mackerel, but unfortunately a thousand men with spearguns could have impacted an environment as delicate as this one. To Mauricio though, spearfishing was a part of his life and he wanted the Caymanian government to make allowances for that fact, exactly the way they did for locals. It was a substantial ethical debate, and exactly the sort of thing we liked to hash out as we glided through the darkness.

And, because we were men, we also liked to speak of women. Susan, Mauricio's fiancé was more than good for him. She was his rock, an intelligent, strong woman, and exactly what Mauricio needed. She was older, in her forties to his 32, but she gave him foundation and direction. Mauricio was the type of guy who was all sky and water while Susan was more grounded in the here and now. They filled in each other's blanks perfectly. Susan was blonde, about five feet four inches, and in very good shape, wearing her age like a soft and lovely patina. She and Mauricio had met when they were in Hawaii and, like me, they were eager for a transfer when the Cayman job came open.

On the morning of January 14th, 2002, Susan was scheduled to work offshore where the big tourist sub, The Atlantis, was diving. It was a gorgeous morning, clear and warm, so Mauricio decided to walk with her to the dock and help her onto the launch that would take her out to the dive site. Before stepping on board to leave him, she lovingly looked back at him, brushing a stray hair from his forehead.

"Do you know what you want for dinner tonight?" she asked.

Mauricio shrugged. "No, not really. I'll have whatever you're having. As long as you do the cooking." He smiled at his own joke.

"Okay," she said softly, "I'll figure something out." She studied the sunlight on his hair and basked for one more moment in the warmth of his energy beside her. "I love you, you know," she said.

"I love you, too" he replied, and leaning down, he kissed her cheek and helped her get on the launch. The motor roared to life, and as the boat pulled away, they watched one another grow smaller with distance and waved a silent goodbye.

I had plans to go diving with Mauricio at twelve o'clock sharp that day, but I had errands to run, it was miserably hot, and time seemed to be dragging. As I stood in a frustrating line at the bank, the big brass clock above the tellers' cage warned me that it was just minutes until noon and I would never make it out to meet Mauricio on time. Since I was already late, I decided to turn my attention to finishing the errands. I'd just have to catch up to him sometime later in the day.

When Susan came knocking at my door about 5:00, I

thought nothing of it. I simply saw a familiar face through the doorway, waved at her and opened up with a "Hi" as she stepped in. If I'd been paying closer attention though, I could have seen the whole story written on her face. Her mouth was fixed in a hard line and she spoke immediately and without any of the usual pleasantries.

"Gary, Mauricio is not at home," she said, her voice far too steady to seem natural. It was the unmistakable sound of pure concern. "His dive gear is nowhere to be found and it's getting late. I am very concerned about him. What do you think we should do?"

Susan had caught me by surprise. I was working on balancing my checkbook when she arrived, so when she first started talking to me, my thoughts were still lingering somewhere on the red ink side of my ledger, rehashing debts paid and debts owed. But as she continued, her eyes caught my attention. They were focused right on mine, looking right through me and down into my very core, as if she could find the answers she urgently needed somewhere inside my head. There had to be some other place Mauricio might be, I said. Had she'd considered the possibility he was wasting time at The Blue Parrot or The Lone Star? Or maybe he was reading a paper somewhere? She civilly tolerated this inane grilling for a second or two, a rehash of the very same questions she had doubtless asked herself several times before she got up the strength to walk the eternal ten or twelve steps to my door.

I got my blades, wetsuit, and snorkel. We walked down the steps, across the rocky beach and to the water in almost the same silent manner that Mauricio and I had walked to take our first dive. This time, though, my heart was heavy and my mind focused.

It was, by far, the most significant dive of my entire life. Nobody but me knew his local dive sites, and the two of us had covered an awful lot of territory over the last three months. I was fully prepared to search every square inch of it if I had to. Whatever it took. We needed to find Mauricio. As I was striding into the water, Susan called out to me.

"Gary!" she shouted, startling us both with the sharpness in her voice. I turned to see her put a hand over her mouth as if to stop the outburst that said so much about her true mind-set. She took a moment to compose herself, and her tone was again controlled when she finally dropped her hand and choked out, "Do you think I should call someone?"

Saying yes to that question would mean that both she and I knew in our hearts Mauricio was dead, and I wasn't willing to go there quite yet. It was too soon to know for sure what had happened to him and I didn't want to be responsible for anyone thinking the worst. I put my tongue behind my teeth and formed a perfect "n" sound to tell her no.

"Yes," I heard myself say. "Yeah, I think you should." The disappointment I felt in my honest response was excruciating. They were the bitterest words I've ever spoken.

I went out searching alone, and was at sea for I don't know how long. I swam out at five o' clock and, though it felt like days, it was probably only about thirty minutes before a small boat with four volunteer rescue divers arrived to help me search. People in scuba gear somberly lowered themselves into the water, spread out around me, and looked up and down the areas I pointed out where Mauricio and I had liked to dive. We were only a very few eyes, searching a vast sea, so it was inevitable that before long, we were all well out of sight of one another, each one covering his or her own territory in complete isolation. The spatial separation between us really didn't matter that much in the long run, though because we were all on the same wavelength. Every diver was hoping against hope he would find Mauricio, and suppressing the cold fear of what would happen if they did.

In the final stages of sunset, a larger boat pulled up next to me. It was a local emergency vessel filled with even more searchers so plainly, what had started as a one-man search was now a full-scale rescue operation. Realizing the awfulness of that fact left me in tatters. The involvement of the authorities certainly meant more help, but it also meant that Mauricio was now officially in trouble, and a hard pit knotted in my stomach. From above me, silhouetted in the glare of the setting sun, I could see a man wearing a bandanna tied around his head leaning over the edge of the cruiser and calling down to me. He looked exactly like a pirate.

"Hey!" he shouted out in a British accent. "Are you Mauricio?"

"No," I yelled back. "I'm his friend. I'm one of the search party. If you're here to search for him, send your divers down and I can fill them in!"

The pirate looked surprised for a moment, then smiled kindly. "How about if you come up here, instead. I understand you've been searching for quite awhile and you look like you could use a break."

He was right, of course. I'd been diving for nearly an hour now and my legs felt like rubber. I hadn't noticed because I was so keenly focused on finding Mauricio. Everywhere I looked in the water that afternoon, among the sponges on the wall, or out in the open sea, I saw my friend freediving in my mind's eye, his powerful kick gliding him through the very same water we had shared only the day before, and I was always surprised to discover that he wasn't really there. Like every ocean he'd ever encountered, Mauricio mastered the Caribbean as if it was little more than his own, personal swimming pool, and I fully expected his wide, white smile to be waiting for me every time I broke the surface.

"Maybe," I thought as I climbed the ladder into the rescue boat, "Maybe this will all turn out to be a bad dream."

Although I was relieved to see the extra help in these people, the mere fact that they had intruded on my quest so abruptly really disturbed the intense solitude I had purposefully spent the afternoon building around me. They were all strangers to me, and this was such a personal search. I looked around at all their unfamiliar glum faces and wondered, "How caring were you people really? Will you treat my friend with compassion when you find him, or was this just another messy, irritating job to you?"

I was in no position to argue, though. Mauricio needed all the help he could get and so did I. I introduced myself properly to the Pirate who told me his that name was Brian.

"So you're Gary," he said, smiling and handing me a towel to wipe my face. "We were dispatched by Susan and she told us to look out for you. I'm the divemaster on the Manta."

"You talked to Susan?" I asked, wiping water from my face. "How's she doin'?"

Brian twisted his mouth uncertainly and shrugged.

"As well as can be expected, I suppose," he said. "This is a hard thing for her I would imagine." He put his hand on my shoulder and gave it a comforting shake. "Just take a moment to catch your breath, and then you can get right back on it." He patted my back.

"You look like the very devil right now."

Unmistakably, Brian was from England, and kind of rough around the edges, but I liked him instantly. It felt good to know that he │was treating this search with the respect it deserved and I felt an overwhelming sense of relief that the crushing burden I had started out carrying alone was now being shared by so many. That's the only way any man can ever manage to survive for long, I suppose. We all need support.

After a moment of rest and a conference with Brian, we started trolling the water at potential dive sites, sailing along as slowly as possible and combing the sea's surface. Brian spread out some more scuba divers too, about 50 feet apart, each with strict instructions to go all the way to the bottom whenever it was humanly possible to do so, and if they couldn't see underwater, they were told to feel their way around the area. After the first pass, it was nearly dark, and no one had found a thing. It was clear that conventional searching was fast becoming futile, but it occurred to me that with a lighted submarine, the gathering dusk would lose its power over us and we could cover more and deeper territory than a few humans with masks and fins ever could. If Mauricio was anywhere above 100 feet, we would have found him by now.

I asked Brian for his cell phone to call the operations manager at work. Dispatch had just heard that Mauricio was missing, and they had exactly the same idea I did.

"Let's launch the sub, then" I said. I'm coming in now and I need two people to go down with me. See who you can round up for me, okay?"

Night had fallen completely by the time I arrived on shore, and it was time to admit that if Mauricio wasn't drunk in a bar somewhere, inexplicably clad in a wetsuit and buying drinks for the house, he was never coming back. The best I could hope for now was to find his body quickly and bring it home before it was too late. In this life, there could be nothing worse than loosing a loved one, and never finding their body again, never being able to see them one last time, or to know for certain how or why they had to die. That kind of loss leaves a hole in your life deeper than any ocean trough. My inner voice told me that it was crucial that a person who was close be the person to bring him home; for Susan's sake and for his family's sake.

But finding a body in the ocean was no small task, especially when it was so close to the drop-off of the Bartlett Deep and the clock was ticking. Mauricio liked to dive on the edge that falls to 6000 feet, so his body could have been almost anywhere; hung up in a coral reef on it's rise to the surface, resting on a haystack, or simply lost in the enormity of the sea. It just so happened though, that this night, the sea was entirely still, an unheard of phenomenon off Grand Cayman Island on a

January evening. There was no real current to speak of, and virtually no wind, so the water was as smooth and clear as blue glass both on top of and below the surface. It was a genuine anomaly, but a miraculous one because it gave us a fighting chance of locating Mauricio's body soon. Most likely, he hadn't been swept away just yet. We still had hundreds more feet of depth to cover though, and there were a great many other factors to consider, like the sea creatures that were just beginning to rise towards the surface looking for food. At least we knew where he wasn't, and at 8 o'clock, we had the sub launched and ready to finish the quest we had started three, endless hours before.

The promised crew of two arrived right on time but, when I saw who was approaching me on the dock, my heart sank. The first crewman was another pilot who had volunteered for the search, a skilled diver that I knew well and I was glad to see him as he shook my hand solemnly before crawling down the hatch and positioning himself by the view port. The third crewmember, however, was Susan. On the one hand, I knew exactly why she wanted to come. Not more than thirty minutes before, I myself had been wracked with frustration because I wasn't out actively searching for Mauricio, and I'm certain that Susan had that very same need to do something proactive in his name. This search was probably all she had. On the other hand, I knew that going down to look for Mauricio was going to be too much for her to bear. No matter how sincerely I wanted to accept and accommodate her needs, I knew that having her on board was going to make it extremely hard for me to stay focused, and possibly even sacrifice the end that I wanted for this sacred mission. Instantly, I buried my feelings and reached out to squeeze her hand as she got in.

"Are you sure about this?" I asked, pleadingly. "I know you feel like you need to do something, but Susan, going down like this on a search, it's gonna be so hard if we find him . . ." I let the sentence drift off. It was an awkward thing to say and I didn't want to say anything more.

"I just want to be near Mauricio," she assured me with a pat on the back of my hand. I released her, and she got into the sub. We descended without delay, all of us staring out into the nighttime sea, scouring it all, from five feet below to five hundred, each one trying to ascertain for certain what every shadowy shape in front us could be. Though I had taken the sub down this way hundreds of times before, this night, there was a terrible twist to the proceedings. Whenever the sub's light hit something on the wall that even vaguely resembled a human being, something like a pair of tube sponges that could be legs for example, Susan would let out a terrified scream. Not just any shriek, but a haunting, wounded sound that absolutely tore me up inside. Here was my friend's fiancé literally mad with pain, and the only thing I could do to help her was to find Mauricio. Sadly, her reaction to the search was preventing me from doing even that.

My instincts had been correct about her ability to handle this, but I couldn't blink. I just had to keep searching until, at last, she looked up at me in the tower with swimming eyes and whispered, "I can't do this anymore, Gary. Please, take me up."

Thank God, I thought, "And may he keep you in the palm of His hand, Susan, but I've got to get this done and I can't do it as long as you're here."

"All right," was all I said.

My relief was palpable when she got out. We had already searched down to 500 hundred feet and I needed weight to descend a bit more quickly than I had while Susan was still in the sub. Fortunately, there were some surface support guys there who fit the bill nicely; two sub techs, one of them a big Honduran man named Jamie, who was just the right size.

"Come on you guys," I urged them. "Hurry up and get in. I know we're close, and I want to find him before it gets too late."

They obediently piled in, and PC 1203 Deep Explorer sank like a stone. In less than five minutes, we were traveling along the wall at 130 feet, It was now ten o'clock when suddenly; Jamie sat upright and said, "Look! There he is!"

"Where?" I asked, looking frantically around me from the tower into the darkness. I couldn't see anything.

"There!" he said with a point, "He's right in front of us."

I must have been totally insane from adrenaline and denial, because, I swear to God, I couldn't see anything but the Sponge belt and the Wall.

"Where," I hissed angrily, "Goddamnit, Jamie. Where do you see him?"

"Gary," he said with extraordinary softness, "He is right in front of your face."

It was Mauricio I was looking at all right, but it wasn't. His face was right in front of mine, his dive mask full of blood. His fins were up and his head was down, his hands limply floating behind him.

I gasped, "Aw, Jesus Christ . . ." I whimpered, and twisted my head away. Even though I had been expecting to find him like this for hours now, I couldn't believe what I was seeing. My friend Mauricio, young, audacious, and, I'd always thought, completely invincible, was dead. It couldn't have been. But there he was. The sea had won again, the way it always did, and I let out a howl of pain.

From below, Jamie said, "Take it easy, Gary. Take it easy. At least you found him. That's what really counts. You did the very best you could."

He was right, of course, but somehow, I still felt like I had let Mauricio down. I stifled another sob behind my flat palms, rubbed my wet eyes with them and took a deep, sniffling breath to regain my sense of the present. There were some things in this life you had to accept to endure, and this was one of them.

"I got it. I got it now," I said, "I'm in control." And I was.

In the spotlight, I saw that Mauricio was caught in a gorgeous swathe of color along the wall. It was one of the most beautiful patches in one of the most beautiful undersea gardens I had seen, and it was the perfect resting place for him. His body was encircled in sponges and corals of purple, yellow, orange and green, all glowing like colors from a stained glass window. It was hard to reconcile the horror of my friend's dead face with the beauty around him, but in a moment of revelation, I understood that this paradox is the way of all life in the ocean, and he was utterly at peace with it. The sub's lights instantly began attracting the soup of life: the worms and the squids and eel that set out searching for food, but none of them ever went near Mauricio. He truly was in paradise and no further harm would come to him.

I put the sub about three feet from where his head was and locked my position right onto the wall, just coming ahead ever so slightly, so no current could take us away. Then, I went down to the view port and put the controls between my legs and reached out and touched the glass.

What did you do to yourself, Buddy? I thought over and over again. What did you do?

After a long minute of final communion, I knew it was time to radio up with the news and I reluctantly grabbed the handset.

"This is PC 1203," I said, speaking softly for fear that Susan might be listening on the other end. "We've found Mauricio." There was no easy way to say such a thing, but it needed to be heard, so I spoke up. "Repeat. We have Mauricio."

At the news, the surface rescue dispatched every sub and every rescue vessel involved in the search to a spot in the water directly above the reef where he lay. There was nothing that anyone aboard these ships could really do to help us now, but the congregation itself was a sign of respect, like a dark and silent funeral fleet. When one of the other subs came down near my own, it looked to my fevered mind like it was genuflecting before the scene and it pleased me immensely to see it. Mauricio deserved all of this and more. But then, there was a voice over the UWT that I would never forget.

"Okay, Gary," it said, "Now that you've got him, just mark

the place. Come on in and we'll get him tomorrow."

I wished I could describe the fury that filled me at that moment, but all I could say was that my mind went scarlet with rage. Again, I took a long, deep breath to compose myself, grabbed the handset with a white-knuckled grip and handed the microphone down to Jamie.

"Here," I said, "I want you to call those bastards back. Call them and tell them that they need to send some divers down here, tonight. We'll wait here all night if we need to, or do whatever it takes, but now, you make good and Goddamn sure that they all get down here tonight." I would die before I left Mauricio's body to the monster.

"Roger that," came the answer from above. It seemed no one wanted to argue.

While we waited, we stayed locked in position, quiet and depleted, all of us trying not to look at Mauricio any more than we had to. It was a matter of respect. For distraction, we sometimes discussed the activity of some brittle stars on a little coral-covered ledge of rock situated directly below the body. It was the best way we knew to allow Mauricio some dignity in his death, focusing on the living world. The brittle stars seemed completely uninterested in the drama around them. Every once in a while, my eyes would wander up and see Mauricio again, and I'd have to re-battle tears from lids that were already scalded with grief, and immediately look away again. With each of these glances, it became more and more evident that concentrating on the life around the corals instead of the corpse of my friend was the right thing to do.

One feature of Mauricio that I did notice on those stolen glances though, was the fact that he still had his weight belt on. During all of our dives, I had always watched Mauricio's hands very carefully, knowing that, as soon as he took them away from that buckle, he was confident he would make it again to the surface. He had always planned to release it if he was ever in trouble, and surely there would never be trouble bigger than this, but still, there was the belt, buckled and firmly in place. It was a beautiful sight, because it meant that, at the moment of his death, Mauricio didn't have time to struggle, think, or take self-preservation measures of any kind. He was simply swimming, alive and conscious one second, and then gone the next. I have since learned that's how shallow water blackout almost always strikes, instantly, and without warning. Its presence told me that Mauricio had died the peaceful sort of death we all long for, doing what he loved to do, and there were no words to explain the comfort the position of that seemingly unimportant belt has given me over the years.

After what turned out to be the longest forty-five minutes of my life, two scuba divers finally swam into view of the bubble. One of them was the head diver of the entire search party; a youthful woman from Canada named Erica. There was a rhythmic grace in her fins as she paddled down towards us and her long blonde hair trailed on the current. That, and the care with which she approached Mauricio's body, gave the whole scene outside my window a fairy-tale quality. She stopped before touching him though, and looked directly at me inside the sub. Behind her mask, her eyes were questioning. She wanted to know something and she made an "okay" sign with her hand to ask, "Is it okay if I take your friend?"

That was good. I was glad she asked and I gave her the okay. As she and Brian respectfully took hold of the body and carried it out of sight, an overwhelming wave of relief washed over me. The work was done. It was time, at last, to surface.

When we got back to pierside, I got out and watched numbly as the crane lifted my sub up and out of the water. The raising and the lowering of the Deep Explorer was always quite a spectacle, even though I'd seen it every working day of my life, and there was comfort in its familiarity. When it was done, I turned to walk away thinking I was alone and found myself instead, surrounded by every single working colleague I had; All the pilots, the maintenance techs and everyone who'd been a part of the search for Mauricio. We were all just standing there, staring at each other with silent concern. With a miserable laugh, I realized that it was me and my pain, not the sub, that had been the true spectacle of the moment, and then, I just let it all go. Sobs wracked me from the back of my spine right out of my throat.

I can only imagine how uncomfortable my friends must have felt as they stood there, each person taking a turn offering me a handshake or an embrace while I struggled to pull myself together. I didn't want to cry, but I was too tired to fight it anymore. It was at least a minute or two before my composure returned, and after the tears, I felt cleansed, clearer, and I think everyone else was grateful for the moment of release, too. But now, standing wordlessly on the dock, there was an obviously empty space among our ranks and all of us began wondering what to do next. We'd never lost a co-worker before. Finally, someone asked the question we were all thinking.

"What do you guys want to do about tomorrow?" he said. "I

mean, we just lost a friend, and we've all lost a partner, so maybe we should just close down for the next day or two. What do you think?"

Superficially, it sounded like a good idea, but I knew it wouldn't help, and I shook my head." I don't know about you guys," I said, rubbing my neck and straightening my back, trying to demonstrate that, in spite of my grief, I was still thinking clearly. "But, if I have to sit at home and look at four walls all day tomorrow, I'm gonna go nuts. I think that getting on with life is the probably only real antidote to a nightmare like this." I looked around to size up how my opinion was going down. "Is anyone else on the same page with me?"

Heads nodded, and without much further discussion, it was decided that we would all report to work tomorrow. Another day, another dollar, thank the good Lord.

At long last, it was time to go home, and as I approached my door at the apartment, I heard a familiar voice outside my door and in the courtyard. I ran my fingers through still damp hair in sudden surprise, just realizing that, even without Mauricio, Susan was still going to be living next door to me. Her door was open, and light was pouring out of her front room onto the stoop. I looked in. Susan was on the phone, but she motioned me in.

". . . Well, that's all I know at the moment, but I'll call you when the plans are all settled," she was saying into the phone. She sounded very calm. I guess now that she knew for certain what had happened to Mauricio, she could accept it. Like Emily Dickinson said, "After great pain a formal feeling comes."

"Yes I will," Susan assured the person on the other end of the line. "And you, too. Take care. I'll call you soon. "

She hung up and opened her arms in an invitation for me to step inside them. She hugged me for a long time, and I heard her voice break as she said into my ear, "I am so sorry for you. He really thought highly of you."

"How did you know we found him? "I asked when, at length, I pulled back from her embrace.

She wiped her eyes. "I was on the balcony with a girl friend when I heard all the radio chatter going off, so no one had to tell me."

She walked to the coffee table, took a sip of water from a tumbler resting there, and swallowed hard. "I just knew." She put the glass back down and walked around the table to sit on the couch, patting the seat cushion next to her.

"Come here and sit down here for a second, Gary. I want to talk to you," she said.

I did as I was told, and once I was settled, Susan looked at the floor for a long silent while, rubbing her hands together and trying to choose her words carefully before uttering a sound. "Listen, Gary," she said at last, raising her eyes to meet mine. "I know that you were supposed to go diving with Mauricio at noon today."

My heart fell. If she knew it, she must surely blame me, and I wanted to jump up right then and interrupt her with a shout, and tell her she didn't have to bother with laying any more guilt on me because I was already swimming in it. I'd blamed myself for this whole tragedy at least once a minute since it began, and my eyes grew hot with grief and shame.

"I know that you feel bad about not going, but you've just got to believe this, Mauricio's death is not your fault." She grabbed my hand for emphasis, squeezing it with every word and lowering her face into the path of my downcast gaze. "Mauricio was the one who decided to go alone. He didn't have to make a decision like that, but he did, and you had absolutely nothing to do with it."

I grimaced, nodding. "I know you're right, but, all day I just kept thinking that the reason he was alone in the first place was because I was too busy to go with him." My voice was very thin.

"Oh, Gary, Mauricio is dead because he went out alone, not because of something you did." She looked out into the room at nothing in particular and shook her head "no" at all the unimaginable events that had come to pass in the last few hours. "Look," she said, turning her eyes back to me, "I can't do anything to bring him back, but maybe I can stop you from carrying around some foolish, misplaced guilt for the rest of your life. This is not just me telling you, this is Mauricio telling you, and anyone with eyes to see the truth telling you, what happened today was not your fault, okay?"

"Okay," I said, smiling to please her.

Two new faces appeared at her door, and she beckoned them in. They were just a few of the many people that would be filtering in and out of her bungalow for days to come and I was satisfied that she wouldn't be alone, so I said goodnight and went down the walk and into my room.

Once inside, I showered and collapsed into bed, totally exhausted. Laying in the dark, I feared I would never be able to sleep again for rehashing the day's nightmare over and over in my mind, but mercifully, that was the last conscious thought I had before I fell into the most tranquil night's sleep of my entire life. For nine long hours, I felt as if I had the wings of an angel wrapped around me, adrift in a peace beyond understanding and a rejuvenation that soothed my guilt and grief shattered brain. Some call that kind of rest "the sleep of the innocent".

The research subs were operating as planned the day after Mauricio's death, and when I came up from my final dive that afternoon, one of the technicians who worked with me, a lanky, dark headed man named Wayne, said that a detective had come by looking for me. Wayne patted down his own pockets, searching for, and eventually, producing a business card with a message on it. Apparently, this Officer wanted me to come by the Coroner's office to identify Mauricio's body. It was about two o'clock in the afternoon, and I had been diving since early that morning. After yesterday's torment, I felt tried and beaten-up, and the very last thing I wanted to do was to go through the agony of seeing Mauricio's body again, but it occurred to me that, if I did the ID, perhaps they wouldn't call Susan and I could spare her that bit of pain, so I headed out.

What I didn't know was that the same detective had already telephoned Susan with an identical request to view the body at just about the same time he'd been by to see me. Susan told me later she was puzzled by the call, because she had been there when they pulled Mauricio out of the water and had identified his body to another policeman before it was sent away in the ambulance. She assumed that this new request must have to do with an official ID of some kind or to maybe to sign some documents. All either one of us knew for certain was that we were both extremely surprised to find the other entering the hospital at exactly the same time, for exactly the same purpose.

We stated our business at the reception area, and were escorted to a little seen part of the building where we were asked to sit on uncomfortable metal chairs in a stark waiting room. There was nothing in the room to look at, nothing to do, and nothing to say between Susan and I that hadn't already been said. There was however, plenty of time to think as we endured an exceptionally long wait. Naturally, I began to wonder what was really going on here. Why would a police detective ask Susan and me to come here and ID a body we had both clearly identified, in front of innumerable witnesses, only the night before? Besides being cruel and unnecessary, it just didn't make any sense. But then, I thought, "When does a bureaucracy ever make any sense or have any heart?"

I was letting my imagination run away with me. This whole process was probably typical, government red tape, and nothing more.

That's when the coroner arrived.

"You can come in now," he said, gesturing with a sweep of his hand to show us which way to go. At the steel door to the room that held Mauricio, I peered through the small, wire re-enforced glass window and didn't want to go in. After my time on the sub yesterday, I had already seen enough of death to last forever, but of course, I wasn't about to let Susan go in and face this task alone. As the door swung open, I saw a man, obviously the detective who had summoned us, waiting next to a sheet-draped body on a gurney, the only two occupants of the otherwise empty, white tile room. The Officer was neat and pressed, a tall, thin Jamaican with high cheekbones and an unsmiling face.

"Are you Gary?" he asked, accenting the "y" in his native lilt.

I said I was. There were no "How do you dos" or sympathy handshakes from this guy. He simply beckoned.

"Come here," he said.

If I had any doubts before, I had none now. The officer was clearly investigating something, I hesitantly walked into the room. It has never crossed my mind that anyone could ever think Mauricio's death was anything other accidental and I reeled at the idea that someone could be questioning whether I was involved in the death of my friend. Just seeing Mauricio was going to be tough enough. I had desperately wanted to keep the image of him floating peacefully among the corals and sponges as the last one I had of my friend. Adding the suspicions of an apparently soulless detective to this stress made me feel as if my legs would surely buckle and I would pass out. But I couldn't. I had to stay strong.

Since my every reaction was evidently being evaluated, I stiffened, standing as tall and as confidently as I possibly could. My bravado worked right up until the officer moved his dark hand over the sheet, and abruptly pulled it back.

Gone was the illusion of the final dive. There was no paradise here, only death. Mauricio was stiff with rigor mortis, lying on a cold, steel slab, and I slumped and wept. Susan collapsed onto my shoulder, grabbing me for comfort. The detective remained impassive.

"Yes, that's him," Susan said. I covered her with my arms to protect her from further ordeal. The officer turned his attention to me, and started asking questions you would think no feeling person would want to ask at a moment like this but which I am sure were purely routine for him.

Could I give him an account of my whereabouts at all times yesterday he wanted to know? Did I have any corroborating witnesses to those whereabouts? When was the last time I saw Mauricio alive? What sort of a relationship did I actually have with my friend? I answered all of these questions honestly, but was left with the impression that the detective wasn't buying my story. The feeling of being suspected played into the maelstrom of my emotions and anger rose to the surface. It was all I could do to control myself.

The next week, there was memorial service at sea, and the detective showed up again, this time with some woman in tow. It could have been his wife, or girlfriend, or, maybe, it was another female officer. I could have cared less who she was. It seemed to me that the only reason she could be there was to double check how we were all reacting and it galled me to think that, officially, there was still some doubt over the circumstances of Mauricio's death. I could taste the bitterness provoked by the presence of the uninvited couple and right then I could cheerfully have executed the one quick bump it would take to knock the two of them overboard. It occurred to me that this was not exactly the nicest thing to think at a funeral. The idea this afternoon was to forgo tears and anger to concentrate, instead, on laughing and sharing happy memories in an effort to celebrate, not grieve, the life of Mauricio Solis. I resolved then, that despite the unwelcome presence of the Officer and his companion, I would honor my friend this day how I damn well wanted to.

Friends gathering to share their fond memories of someone's life was an idea that would have appealed to anyone, especially Mauricio, but as we approached the dive site, it became increasingly apparent that the "celebration" part was far easier supposed than accomplished. When a thirty-one year old man, the father of a ten year old boy, and a life force of hurricane proportions had died, it was awfully hard to find something to celebrate, even though we all shared stories about him that made us all smile.

When we were directly over the dive site where Mauricio lost his life, Susan handed me a huge wreath of flowers, and said, "Here, Gary. I want you to toss these into the water. I had the florist make them up special for you. It's a friendship wreath and it's yours to honor Mauricio with."

I smiled, accepted her touching gift and started tossing the flowers with an anesthetized mind, a trick I had learned over the past week whenever it hurt too much to think, but even though I had my sunglasses on, it was obvious to Susan that I was crying, the one thing I wasn't supposed to be doing that day. She put a hand on my shoulder to stop me, and said softly, "Please don't get upset. We want to keep this a celebration, remember?"

But I couldn't. I just couldn't hold back the tears anymore. For a solid week I had kept it all in, putting a lid on my emotions every time a negative thought even crossed my mind. I kept them suppressed for Susan, or Officer Best, or because I didn't want to upset anyone around me. Now, though all those same reasons were here in force, I had chosen this moment to lose my mind. I remember thinking God, I can't stop this, as I wept and tossed flowers. There were so many flowers in that damn wreath; it seemed to go on forever. Finally, in rage, I flung the wreath into the water whole, and for the first time since the night Mauricio died I started sobbing.

Susan pleaded with me. "Please stop, Gary. This day is not about that."

I wanted to stop with all my heart but all I could manage to say was, "Susan, I can't do this any other way."

My tears began setting other people off, and I could feel Susan starting to crumble as I systematically ruined her celebration. Then, from the middle of the crowd, a woman pushed her way forward. It was Erica, the woman who had recovered Mauricio's body. She walked right up to me and, without a word, put her arms around me, hugged me tightly, and led me off. When we were away from the crowd, I returned her squeeze in a limp manner because I hardly knew the girl, and I certainly didn't want to embarrass her or anyone else more than I already had. But still, I was hurting.

She stopped her embrace, looked at me sternly and demanded, "No. I want you to hug me!" and as she wrapped me tightly in her arms and clung to me, I felt her caring concern pass right through me, and into my spirit. My tears slowed, then stopped, and all the pain went away. All I had ever needed was just one person to recognize that, even though Mauricio and I were new friends, I had come to care for him like a brother and that the loss of his life was devastating to me. Her simple, human, touch was so special, and so needed, that it took away the very last of my despair.

Mavis told me that there were people in this world called "energy healers," men and women born with such a gift for empathy that, in a single touch, they could heal others. I thought that perhaps there were such people, but there's no real mystery as to why their touch can heal. Deep inside, we all have the capacity to be healers. The trick to having a healing touch, I thought, didn't lie in some genetic mishap or God-given gift. It's nothing more than being able to see and aid other people's misery, instead of being utterly blinded by your own. It would have been very easy for Erica and Brian to miss the service that day. They were two busy people dealing with their own grueling problems and they certainly didn't have to be there. No one was expecting them. They didn't even know Mauricio, but from the moment they brought him to the surface, they could see what his death had done to the people around him and they decided to reach out and help in any way they could. It was a decision that meant everything to me.

The place where Mauricio had worked in Hawaii was having another wake for him on the same day and in Mexico, at that moment, there was also a simultaneous memorial service for him there. On two different oceans, in three different parts of the world, a host of people all gathered to celebrate his life because, as I said, this was a man of charisma; someone who loved easily and was easy to love. It was our devotion to him that brought us together and made us all "energy healers" for one, sunny Caymanian afternoon.

Of course, the detective was watching it all. I tried to interact with him at different stages of the service to see if he had changed his mind about his suspicions of the circumstances of Mauricio's death, but his responses were still stiff and guarded. He was determined to do his job and check out every person who was involved with Mauricio's or might know something about his death, and it appeared that still include me.

Some days later, I got a call from him. He wanted to interview me and Susan one more time. The Officer began scribbling notes as he talked to us. It was a while after the accident by this time, and I had grown weary of being polite to the detective. He asked me again, "So, Gary. Do you remember exactly what day it was that this all happened?"

I sighed and said, "Yes, I do, Officer Best. It was January 14th."

His voice came across as acerbic. "Man. You've certainly seem to have got that date etched in your mind."

I threw my hands up, glared at him in helpless indignation and spluttered "Of course I damn well do. It's not every day it happens, losing my friend like that."

He was silenced, but still made a note about my answer but as he started to ask his next question, the phone rang. Susan answered it, then held the receiver out in a limp hand towards the officer.

"It's for you," she said, interrupting his next question brusquely. The detective walked over, picked up the phone and grunted his name as a greeting. He listened intently to a mumbling voice we could barely hear in the silent room.

"Do you know that for sure?" he asked when the mumbling stopped. Susan and I exchanged wary glances. Somehow, we knew the call was about Mauricio.

"I see," he said at the incoherent response, and for the first time since I had met him, his face softened a bit. He looked over at where I was sitting. "No, no" he added, "That's fine, and thanks. That's all I need to know." He punched the "end call" button and set the receiver down, then flipped his little note pad shut, stuffing it in the breast pocket of his starched white shirt.

"That was the coroner," he said. "Mauricio Solis' death has been ruled by him as accidental. There will be formal inquest but no further investigation"

I couldn't help thinking "Well, I hope you're satisfied at last" looking at the policeman through narrowed eyes. Suddenly, I saw a transformation come over him. A veil had been lifted, and the man standing before me now was much different than the one who had answered the phone only a moment ago. Apparently, the detective wasn't a monster, after all; just a man to whom suspicion is a necessary part of his daily job. All he wanted was to ensure laws were upheld and justice was done on this Island that had been a paradise during his childhood. To my disgrace, it never occurred to me through my suffering that he too, might be a human being dealing with an appalling and emotional situation but forced by his duties to remain detached and inquisitorial.

As he cleared his throat and went on talking, all my anger and indignation at what I had considered his insensitive behavior to me, and Susan, fell away. I now felt gratitude that people like this detective existed in this world and a twinge of guilt that I had been too wrapped up in my own emotions to see that, in his own way, this man had wanted to make sure right was done by my friend.

There was a court hearing a few months later and because I had found the body, I was summoned to testify at the formal court inquest. Caymanian courts had adopted English court procedures so the magistrate judge wore a white curled wig and black robes. Stepping into the witness box was like stepping back to another century. The judge who oversaw the proceedings was a large woman of Jamaican heritage with an understanding demeanor who wrote down every word I said. I was grateful for her sensitivity, but it didn't make up much for the fact that, with the pounding of a rubber stamp or two, the entire episode of Mauricio's death was over, as if you can file away a human life just like that.

But fortunately, nothing on Grand Cayman was ever finished for me until Mavis had her say. She watched me mope around the apartment for several more weeks after the inquest was closed, and I could tell by the lines in her forehead that she was worried about me. Everything about Mavis was usually warm, Caribbean sunshine, from the large colorful housedresses she wore to her broad, bright, smile, so I hated to be the source of her distress, but in my own house, I had to be able to complete my grief unabated. I was sitting, reading, and brooding one beautiful afternoon when I heard her

Caymanian lilt behind me.

"It was a mistake you know, Mister Gary," she said.

"What was?" I asked, putting my book down and turning in my chair to look at her. I thought perhaps she had broken something I owned and actually thought I would give a damn.

"Your friend's death," she said.

I snorted. "I know it was," I said, smiling sardonically and turned back to my reading.

"No really," she said, walking over in front of me, to ensure my attention, "It was. The other night, I said the Lord's Prayer and lit candles to call out to La Sirene."

La Sirene was a consort of Agwe's, also called the Queen of the Sea. The spirit of La Sirene was sometimes seen as a whale, but most often, she appeared as a beautiful woman with long hair and the tail of a fish. It was La Sirene that was responsible for all the intangibles of the sea; things like its beauty, its power, its movement, and its magnetism. She was the mother of all the sea creatures, and she protected her own fiercely.

Mavis continued. "I put out some shells and white rum and a picture I have of a deep blue sky with a gold moon and sun, and I offered her a yellow melon as a sacrifice. Then La Sirene came to me in a dream."

I leaned forward in my chair. "What did she say?" I asked.

"She said she thought Mauricio was one of her children. He'd been down in that deep so many times, and he hunted like a fish and could breathe like a fish, and he had those long, slim fins that moved him so fast, she thought he was her own. That day, when he wanted to come up, La Sirene didn't let him because she thought he belonged to the sea. She didn't know it would hurt you and everyone else this much. To her, it was the right thing to do, keeping him where he was content." She shook her head. "I tell you Mr. Gary, I think it was all a terrible mistake."

I smiled at her. "I don't think that Spirits make mistakes, Mavis," I said. "Even if it doesn't look fair to you and me, maybe La Sirene knew exactly what she was doing all along."

Mavis' smile returned. "You think so?"

"Maybe," I said, and walked over to the window and looked out at the sea. I knew that, somewhere in the waters of the Caymanian rectangle, the spirit of Mauricio was still gliding, and that our paths would one day cross again in it's odd and beautiful world. They just had to. I'd already encountered so much down there in the form of bent drop plates, the ghostly lights at the Kirk Pride, and the creature from the cave, that I knew Mauricio must be waiting there to see what would happen to me next. Sadly, my next adventure would not be a happy one. Another of Sirene's tragedies was about to unfold.

6

Passing time and searingly emotional events had separated me from that day I got "lost" with Jason and encountered the unknown, unseen monster that shifted 800lbs. of drop tray weight with one hit. Life, however, was about to bring me and the little sub back into its orbit.

The first time I met Penny Allen and Tom Fitz from the BBC's Natural History unit I had just finished a long, exhausting day diving with a large French film crew that included Umberto Pelizzari, the world record freediver. Umberto was a vibrant man who, to say the least, was someone who believed, "There is a limit to everything, except, that is, human beings". He was making a series about the ocean called L'Odyssee Bleu and it was an intense shoot. I was relieved when he finally decided to call it a day. It was five o'clock in the evening, and I had just enough time to take the launch to shore for a moment of rest before I had to start the dive process all over again with the BBC. They were making a program about the Oceans which was called Blue Planet and wanted to follow Dr Eugebie Clark down the Cayman wall in search of the huge Six-gill sharks she had seen. They wanted them on film for their program to amaze and educate the viewing public. They had already been through two pilots, and I was their last chance at getting a Six-gill on film. Tired as I was I was excited to be working with these talented people as well as searching for one of the candidates for my mystery monster.

I had made arrangements days before with a local fisherman named Ferris for a tuna as close to 60 lbs. as he could possibly manage to catch, and he outdid himself, delivering a 65 pounder right on cue; a feat that still amazed me. Ferris was part of a small, native community nearby that traveled far out to sea alone in traditional Jamaican fishing canoes, a narrow type of craft that was once lovingly fashioned by hollowing out trees. These days, trees were at a premium on Grand Cayman, so fiberglass had to suffice. The fisherman looked mighty small as they disappeared over the horizon in the little boats, but they rarely failed to come back laden with fish. Ferris had labored for two long days to find just the perfect catch for me and he proudly presented it as I arrived on the harbor.

"Good God, Ferris, she's a beauty," I said, whistling through my teeth as I tied up the launch. The fisherman beamed with pride.

Ferris and his friends had also been providing me with the guts and heads of their catches for the last two weeks so I could pre-bait the rectangle for the BBC crews. The water had been scarlet with chum for days in order to attract as many big sharks as possible. While most sane folk would know to stay away from a pre-baited area like that, a "booze cruise" tourist ship called the Jolly Roger, a replica of Columbus' Santa Maria, had been sailing near my precious blood-slick just a day or two before. It seemed that a drunken crew member of the Roger had been left behind on shore that night and decided to row out to the ship on a dingy and salvage his job. Unfortunately for him, dark thick clouds and strong winds, not to mention a pint or two of rum, prevented the man from finding his target, and he was lost at sea. I fully expected he would turn up as a snack for my prey, but Ferris had disappointing news for me.

"They found that sailor on a Venezuelan freighter last night, you know," he said.

I smiled wickedly. "Oh, that's too bad. Guess I won't be able to tie his old carcass to the crash bar, after all. I'll have to depend on this fish instead."

We shared a good laugh.

Diving to bait a Six-gill was extremely tricky business because it's almost impossible to land large bait correctly in the total darkness of the deep. As a hunting pilot descended, he had to be mindful not only of the darkness and the jagged haystacks, but of the fact that he had a tuna the size of a goat tied to the sub's crash bar, trailing at will on the current around him. When he landed, he had to situate his sub safely of course, but first, he had to set the bait down, directly in front of the view port, so the cinematographer could have a good shot at any action the tuna might draw in.

Dave, who'd been the first pilot for the BBC team, accidentally overshot the mark on landing, so his tuna went sailing, in a graceful, slow motion catapult right over the wall, and down into the deep. Any feeding that took place on that dive was well out of range of the cameras. And Biff, being Biff, actually ran into the 800-foot haystack during his plunge with the British crew. To be fair, he'd only hit the stack because the freshly killed tuna he was trailing had doubled back on its line and run smack into the sub's vertical thruster, flinging Tuna blood and guts everywhere. The dung literally hit the fan, and the gore all but blinded him. Unable to see through the bloody mess, he had no landmarks to guide by, and since he was moving at a pretty good clip when the sushi started flying, it was inevitable that the sub would eventually collide into a stack. At the sound, everyone inside looked at Biff with large, pleading eyes.

Among the crew on that particular voyage was an elderly scientist named Roger who had seen it all in his long and illustrious career. The dive with Biff was the last he ever did. He retired the next day, sending Dr. Penny Allen in his place for the trip with me, a decision that had left me forever in his, and Biff's debt.

My quick jaunt to the shore was a success. I had an empty bladder, a boat full of snacks from Foster's Food Fair, and a big-ass tuna for bait. I couldn't have been more eager to get started on the project ahead. I hopped into the launch, fired up the outboard, and headed out to the dock where two solitary slim figures, Penny Allen, a marine biologist, and cameraman Tom Fitz, were patiently waiting for me in the dwindling sunlight. After the hustle and bustle of the huge French crowd, I'd expected a much more elaborate undertaking than this unassuming crew of two I saw smiling and waving in my direction. I waved back uncertainly and headed over to pick them up.

"That's all you have?" I thought as I pulled the boat alongside the wharf. Sitting at their feet was scarce equipment, nothing more than a camera and a monitor really, and it took me by surprise. As a kid, I had eagerly inhaled undersea documentaries, sprawled on the living room floor with my chin propped on my hands, rapt face bathed in the stark glow of a black and white TV. My entire family marveled at the feats of Jacques Cousteau and his National Geographic cohorts, so it came as a bit of a shock to discover that getting that kind of fabulous footage didn't always require a shipload of rippling-muscled, undersea daredevils with thick accents and cameras mounted inside steel cages. Apparently, folks as unassuming as this pair of quiet, friendly, scientists and even me, in my little jalopy of a sub, must also have been able to capture a spectacle or two on film. It was a pleasant revelation.

The BBC pair may have been low-key, but to me, they were tremendously appealing given the pedigree of their employer and the nature of their quest. Penny was a young woman with what I thought of as a typically English look and style. She was professional but open and friendly and when she smiled she radiated enthusiasm. Tom was also young and his slim built body was clearly abundant in energy. He had a quiet smile permanently fixed to his face but also the keen focus I'd come to recognize as a sign of a man constantly framing shots inn his mind.

"Hello, Gahry," Penny said, rounding the "a" in my name with her perfectly proper English accent. She held out her hand for me to shake in greeting. " I'm pleased to meet you but I'm afraid I've an admission to make. This is my first dive in a submarine. I hope that is not a problem for you."

"No way," I said laughing. "It'll make it all the more fun."

I never saw that one coming: an undersea researcher who had never been deep under the sea. It didn't matter, though. It was always great to descend with someone who had never been below the surface before. You get to see the deep through fresh eyes, like it was your first time down there, too.

"I just hope I can make it a dive to remember and we get something you guys can use on film," I said. "Are you a little nervous?"

"Not at all," she said enthusiastically "I can't wait to get underway."

"Well, let's get on it then," I replied. Even as I was tying up the launch, I could feel in my gut that this dive was going to be something really special. New faces, new techniques, and a dive to find a creature few people had ever seen. This was the stuff I lived for, and I made a silent promise to myself that no matter what difficulties we might face on the descent, by God, I was going to get us all down there, deliver some good footage, and bring us home safely.

But the odds were not in favor of that happening. The surface that night was not calm. In fact, it was rough and getting rougher. The sky had low dark clouds that obscured the sunset, and an occasional flash of lightning revealed the silhouettes of departing ships on the horizon. There was a good-sized storm headed our way, and for this little expedition, that could mean both happiness and misery.

The trouble was, I needed illumination to navigate during our descent and light below the surface could be an extremely tricky thing. The enormous undersea mountain range of the Cayman Islands, the Sierra Miestra, was made up completely of limestone covered by white sea snow, so the Cayman Wall appeared an iridescent blue when first underwater. But, a few feet deeper, the light diminished drastically, making the wall more and more difficult to see. It's fortunate that the surface of the rock was white because it reflected light beautifully on a typical sunny Caribbean afternoon. Some days, even as deep as five hundred feet, divers can actually read the time on their watches without needing a flashlight, an impossible feat in virtually any other ocean around the world. On a night like this one, however, with dark clouds looming ominously overhead, obscuring the last shards of daylight, it would be a miracle if I could see my hand in front of my face after the first hundred feet. Still, we had to travel at night if we were to have any hope of seeing a Six-gill. It's only after sunset that the largest migration of living creatures on this planet begins. Every single night, one thousand million tons of animals rose from the deep ocean towards shallower depths in search of food, and the giant Six-gill rose right along with them.

This tremendous underwater stampede began close to the surface with tiny grazing animals ascending just a few feet to eat the phytoplankton who required sunlight to survive. Little meat-eaters rose next, snapping up the vegetarians in their miniature jaws and stinging tentacles, with larger and larger predators, from deeper and deeper parts of the ocean all following, each one consuming the smaller creatures above them, until you got to the biggest teeth of the largest predators from the bottommost parts of the ocean; Predators like the Six-gill. These sharks ascend from 6000 feet to 1000 feet nightly, using their finely honed eyesight to find any bioluminescent "glow in the dark" signals that some simple-minded prey might have given off. A Six-gill will eat anything that had the courage to light up in front of him. Before over fishing, great schools of pelagics roamed the oceans living a long and full life cycle. The dead fish would fall in considerable numbers to the bottom of the ocean and feed the six gills. Now however, sea life was diminishing and the six gills must work harder and travel farther to eat.

Looking up at the dusky sky, with the clouds blocking even the light from the moon, it occurred to me that the extra gloom might be an unexpected boost to the success of our mission. The darker it was, the more attracted to the bait our Six-gill was probably going to be. A Six-gill's eyes were designed for hunting in the dark, including a "third eye" on the top of its head that measures how far from the surface the shark was swimming. It was simply easier for the shark to see bait in total darkness, and since it was already "Jaws" natural dinnertime, we'd have that much better odds. A moonless, starless night certainly sounded like the key to success, but at this point, the whole thing was a calculated crapshoot with three lives at stake.

The plan was to descend to a haystack that was the steepest

peak available at 1000 feet, as deep as we could go with our particular time and distance limitations. From this spot, the scent of our tuna would be lifted out into the ocean much faster, farther, and deeper than from any other local landing site, and if I put the bait down properly, there would be the added bonus of having a rock immediately behind the shark against which we could judge his size: An ideal stony backdrop for our little stage. The rock was just over twenty feet away, so all the shark would have to do was look into the camera, say, "cheese" and we could examine the footage later to determine the length. It was the best possible site and hereafter, I would refer to it as "Penny's Pinnacle."

It was time to tie the fish to the crash bar using the 20-foot monofilament we had selected. The clear wire would vanish in the water so any action we filmed would look totally natural. I made some fresh cuts in the tuna and they bled nicely.

"That ought to drift out quite a ways when we land," said Penny confidently.

I nodded in agreement, but it was too early to be talking about landing the tuna. I was far more concerned about just finding our way down the wall without crashing into one of the nasty limestone spikes that would be jutting up at us along the way. Free falling through total darkness as we were about to do, with nothing but memory, night vision, and intuition to guide us, the chances were very good that we would hit at least one of them, Biff-style, if we didn't execute every function flawlessly.

"Are you going to have to get into the water to tie the fish off?" asked Penny.

Someone was going to have to do it, but I really didn't want to be the one to get wet.

"God, I hate to," I said. "I don't want to sit in wet clothes for hours on end."

I looked at the support guys beseechingly, but neither of them was too keen on hanging out in damp shorts, either.

The answer was obvious; one of us would just have to strip down and hop into the water in the buff. I didn't know who it would be but I did know it wasn't going to be me. I could see the support guys were being made uncharacteristically bashful by Penny's presence so I encouraged her and Tom to get into the sub and as soon as they were installed I worked to convince the support guys that she couldn't see anything and wouldn't look.

The support guys exchanged wary glances and there was a lot of pier-kicking deliberation. Finally, one of the guys twisted his mouth into a "what the hell" expression, shrugged and said, "All right. I'll tie off the damn fish."

Tom and Penny had already gone down the hatch to find their places in the cabin. They nestled in by the bubble and began spreading out their equipment, making certain it was in perfect working order. The camera had to be absolutely trouble-free with plenty of film on hand because there are no second takes at 1000 feet. Tom lifted his camera to his eye and began panning it around to get a feel for the range of view he might expect out of the view port. On the edge of his peripheral vision, to the right hand side, he could detect some lively pink and gold flickering in the water just above him. He pointed the camera upwards, then took the lens away from his eye to clearly see what it was. The motion caught Penny's eye at the same time and she looked up from some reading to see a huge tuna sinking down on a translucent fishing line that led up the bottom half of a scrawny, naked man treading water on the surface. Penny and Tom exchanged glances that blossomed into face-wide smirks. Tom's camera immediately went to his eye and the whirring of film could be heard. The legs of the naked man splashing above them tucked, then his head appeared as he dove down, frog kicking his way across the view port. He struggled to stay under as he tied the fish on the crash bar, and occasionally, his fiercely white ass lost the gravity battle and rose higher than his head. The whole process took almost a minute, and he was obviously in a hurry for breath when rocketed back towards the surface. Tom's camera clicked off.

"Did you get it?" Penny asked.

"Oh yeah," said Tom, putting the camera back down and wiping a smudge off the lens.

Eventually, our gear was all packed and the cameras were mounted to the front of the view port. A last pee was in order and I advised Tom and Penny to do the same. Nine hours is a long time to be down in a confined area with someone who needs to go, and there is nothing more than a zip lock bag for a toilet in the Twilight Zone. The last thing I did before I got into the sub was to take a moment alone to collect my thoughts, visualizing every inch of the descent in my head as clearly as possible. Then, with one deep, cleansing breath, it was time to go.

When we were all safely settled in the sub, I secured the hatch tightly. I radioed to my damp Surface officer aboard "Igor," our mother ship.

"This is PC1203 Deep Explorer. Be advised hatches secure, life support on and running. Briefing complete. Requesting permission to vent and dive."

"Deep Explorer you are clear to vent and dive."

I switched on the oxygen and the scrubber. The sub's antiquated air conditioning system, basically no more than a block of ice and a fan, started up as well and thankfully, the humid interior of the submarine began to chill. The tanks were filling nicely and we started to descend, but as the waterline passed away from the view port, we lost all light very quickly. In the cool, dark comfort of the cabin, I no longer had any excuse for the sweat on my brow other than the fact that I didn't like what I was seeing outside. It was disturbingly dark out there. So threatening, in fact that right away, I did what every well-trained, intelligent pilot does when his vision becomes suddenly and entirely obliterated. I barely suppressed a deep-seated desire to totally freak-out.

What in the name of holy hell do I think I'm doing down here at night? I thought. I can't see a thing in this damn soup. I shook my head in helpless resignation and prayed from the bottom of my heart. God, help us. We're all crazy people on this sub. Please bring us back alive.

Penny and Tom were cooing with enthusiasm below, while I strained to see through the darkness, making out only the vaguest outlines of black on black objects along the wall. I turned on my lights and quickly discovered that they only made matters worse. When using lights in black water, nothing was seen but particles of churning sea snow reflecting back, a phenomenon called backscatter, and it could be very disorienting. I snapped them off instantly, relying instead on my depth gauges and the hundreds of dives I had done before this one, the way a blind man counts his steps and trusts that objects are placed where he expected them to be. I managed to find my way. There was a sonar system available on my sub, but it's almost always best to rely on visual cues. The truth was, Sonar on a small boat like this was somewhat redundant because usually ordinary eye contact can be made with everything when there was sufficient light. The whole submarine wasn't much bigger than a mini van so vision wasn't usually a problem, but I had never been down at night before. Worst of all, we had to light up the whole cabin to use the equipment, and if someone had ever had to flip on the bright bathroom light in the dead of night they knew exactly what that sudden brilliance did to their night vision. I'd been down in this area so many times that I thought I would be able to tell where we were, and it looked as though I could, as long as we were above 200 feet.

At 200 feet, the wall was still barely visible, but descending further, the blackness started getting sinister. We managed to detect a ledge at 250 and went around it, but at 300 feet, the overhang cast a shadow that made it completely impossible to see. We were in real danger, engulfed in what looked to me like a sea of swirling black paint, and for a split second I thought about calling the dive off and surfacing while we still had time. It was an idea that passed as soon as it came, however. It was no secret to anyone on the sub that baiting a Six-gill after dark was going to be risky business, and in a few hundred more feet it wouldn't make that much difference if we were five hundred feet or five miles below the surface. Go deep enough, and it's always dark to human beings. The most compelling reason to keep going, though was the fact that Penny, Tom and I, each for our own reasons, all wanted to find that Six-gill shark the way a drowning man wanted air. If we could just hang in there for a few more minutes, I'd be in an area I knew well enough to navigate blindfolded so we were better off staying the course. I peered out of my tower into the ocean void and flew as I always did, by instinct.

At 400 feet, a miracle happened. An unexpected bolt of lighting from the approaching storm lit up enough of the mountainside, ever so slightly, from the heavens right down into the ocean at our depth. It was a single, merciful, burst of light, but it was just enough to allow me to get my bearings. I mentally marked a familiar structure on the side of the mountain, and immediately felt much more at ease. It was just the mental snapshot I needed to help my eyes to adjust to the darkness and gradually, I began to make out the detail on wall. I exhaled a vulgarity in audible relief, and there was some snickering from below.

Tom and Penny had been quiet up to that point, silently sensing that I needed to concentrate fully on our descent, but at my interjection, Tom took the opening in the tension to ask something that had been bothering him since we launched.

"So tell me, Gary, how many times have you done this before?" He was gazing out the view port, camera in hand, trying to look nonchalant but I knew better. He'd been in the sub with Biff the day before.

My response was a bright one. "Oh . . . this is my first time," I replied.

Tom's head whipped around so fast he looked like a turbo-charged Linda Blair, although in the dark, I couldn't really make out his expression.

"At night," I added with a smile, and then repeated reassuringly, "At night." Tom started breathing again as I said, "It's probably my 400th dive total."

He laughed, and that was the last questioning of my credentials to be heard from this particular crew although I would hear the same question again from thousands of other crews on thousands of other passenger dives. It's awfully hard to resist the temptation to tease anyone who asked, and I couldn't help but wonder why they always waited until they're hundreds of feet below the surface, and at my complete mercy, before they bring it up. I thought that's the kind of question you'd want to ask your pilot before you got into his sub and dropped a half-mile, but maybe that's just me.

We continued to fall silently through the black Caribbean Sea and, one way and another, I managed to coax some shadowy images out of every sensory receptor my poor burning retina, macula, and cornea could spare. I was struggling hard to maintain visual contact with the wall because I had to. Behind us, there was nothing but blackness and 23,600 feet. Any wayward current, or even something as certain as crossing a thermocline, a "bump" in the water where warm and cold currents come together, could have thrown us completely off course. My eyes were completely fixated on the view outside of my tower and I had to actually remind myself to turn them away every so often to check my instruments as we descended. At four hundred and fifty feet, I took a quick glance at the depth gauge and then back out the window. The next glance was at five hundred feet, then five twenty. Each time I turned my eyes away it became more and more difficult for my gaze to readjust and focus properly on the surroundings outside the sub. Five hundred and sixty feet. I sat up in alarm.

"Shit!" I whispered to myself. At least I thought I said it to myself.

Penny and Tom asked in unison, "What's the matter?"

"Gotta slow down," I responded coolly. "We've got Haystacks coming up, and I want to make sure we have time to steer clear."

I might have looked as confident as a judge, but my insides had just turned soft. So far it seemed, no matter how deep we went, it wasn't getting any easier for me to see and at six hundred and forty feet, I knew there were haystacks every-where, as sharp as daggers, just waiting to pierce our hull. I had to make visual contact to avoid them, but I wasn't entirely sure I had allowed the sub adequate time to slow down before we smashed into the first one we came across. A submarine isn't like an automobile. It doesn't exactly stop on a dime. I needed at least sixty feet to slow down enough to avoid a crash but, because I had been about a half a second slow on the trigger at 560, I was afraid we were now falling at too rapid a rate. I couldn't see squat below me, and at six hundred feet, I had my hand on the emergency blow, just in case. Then, out of the darkness below, a triangular shadow began to emerge. It was the tip of the 640 stack, and I knew for a fact we had enough time to slow down and navigate successfully around it. I relaxed the fiery tension in my hand and let go of the emergency lever, shaking my rubbery fingers a couple of times to get the circulation going again. We had just conquered the biggest obstacle on our descent.

"Yahoo!" I yelled, feeling every inch the cowboy. Laughter came from below.

"I take it you like your job?" asked Tom.

"I sure do when everything goes right," I said grinning. "First mission accomplished, Ladies and Gentlemen. We're having to take this whole thing in baby steps because it's so damn dark down here, but we're making good progress. This is the six forty block. Everyone up for a thousand?"

"Absolutely!" said Penny, her tea and crumpets accent making her eagerness that much more emphatic.

I smiled and looked down at the two shadowy figures below me, huddled side-by-side, looking out onto the very last wilderness on earth. I wondered what it was that had brought the three of us together this way; besides the BBC documentary and Roger's retirement, that is. What was the force that could compel three seemingly sane adults to think it was a perfectly reasonable idea to sail out to a couple thousand feet offshore on a dark, stormy night, crowd together in a little metal capsule, and plunge into the choppy sea to a point that's deeper than the highest skyscraper is tall? People should know better than to jump off an underwater cliff in the darkness and fall blindly through a jagged minefield of limestone pyramids on a mission to snap a picture of a huge flesh-eating nightmare, and yet, here we all were, so there must have been something in this pair that made them love the sea the way I did. Once I saw the gospel in our common commitment, I felt a kinship with Penny and Tom that I have never felt with another crew before or since.

My father was the one who had passed his obsession for the sea on to me, and I'm sure that Tom was driven by a similar force in his art. The whole point of The Blue Planet was to assemble images of ocean life that no one had ever recorded before, so Tom's passion to get the shot had to override any fears he may have had about the danger involved if he wanted to get the job done. Tom Fitz already had years of experience of underwater cinematography and had worked on many film projects for the BBC and other wildlife film creators. His ability to capture the magic and wonder of the deep oceans was the perfect culminations of Penny's marine biology researches.

How Penny, with her impeccable academic background, came to be hunting giant sharks in Cayman with us, though, was an altogether unique story. Penny's diversion into the show business that had led her here came while she was doing research on gray seals for her PhD in Marine Biology in London. During a study break one day, she picked up a | magazine called The New Scientist, and leafed through it as she ate her lunch. In the back of the magazine, there was a section of job advertisements, that's pronounced "Ahd-VERT-iz-munts", and, astonishingly, one of the ads was seeking a research assistant on the BBC's new ocean series, The Blue Planet. She nearly choked on her biscuit. Finding an ad like that was a little like opening Variety and seeing "Unknown Actress Wanted for Lead in Upcoming Spielberg Picture. Salary negotiable." It could never happen, and yet, there it was. Some things were just meant to be.

Penny told me later, "I thought, my goodness, what a complete dream job. Everybody in the UK admires the work of the Natural History Unit of the BBC, and David Attenborough in particular. It was something I just thought would be a fantastic thing to do but I never imagined I would be able to because I had no television experience. But the advertisement said they were looking for people with a marine science background and contacts in the marine science world, and I just thought, if you don't apply, you'll never know. I would just spend the rest of my life wondering."

Obviously, she got the job, but I'm pretty sure that the job bought a fair amount of wondering into her life too. As with all those fascinated by the oceans curiosity was a large part of her nature. Wonder, I thought, was what made our lives worth living, and it was certainly what held the passengers of PC 1203 together that night. I was honored to be able to contribute my expertise to achieving the goal Penny and Tom between them had set.

The next depth check was at 800 feet, and fortunately for us all, we'd finally arrived at an area I knew as well as my own back yard. It was still hard to see the landmarks, but in that part of the stacks I could probably find my way around by smell alone. I locked my position on a large rock formation we called "The Wedge," and from there, I turned my heading due south and hopped the sub, like a yellow frog going pad to pad, down to the giant pinnacle known as the 800-foot stack. It was the same rock Biff had bounced off of when he got lost in the blood cloud. I put my lights on the tip of the stack as we approached, and since I knew it was more than

100 feet tall with a sheer, straight face, I followed it down until we arrived at the 900-foot mark. I noticed Tom's tense shoulders relax in relief as we passed it.

"How's it going up there, Gary?" asked Penny from below.

"Almost there," I called back. The big dangers were behind us. My only piloting objective at this point was to slow the submersible down, land the fish and sub, and prevent this boat from being blown off the pinnacle and falling to our crush depth of 1500 feet. PC 1203 might be small, but it had the exact same depth rating as a giant Typhoon-Class nuclear submarine, subs that were about the size of W.W.II aircraft carriers. A Typhoon can cruise along at 1200 feet, just like ours could, but if that same monster machine went down to 1500 feet, the pressure of the sea would crush it like a roach under a boot heel. If the ocean could flatten a piece of equipment the size of a Typhoon, imagine what would become of my poor little Perry Class sub should it ever fall to 1500 feet. Whenever there were four digits on my depth gauge, I make sure to take it nice and easy.

I started the pumps to slow us again, knowing that the landing zone was a small pinnacle, only about 30 feet in diameter, and I needed to be very precise on my touch down. The ratcheting noise of the pumps was loud, and a definite cause to grimace inside the echo chamber of the sub. Penny and Tom covered their ears in distress, but to me, it was a symphony. That clattering meant that the landing we had planned so carefully for the last couple of days was nearly at hand. It was an endearing sound, like an old lawn mower giving it all she's got to get the job done, and I would have gone on reveling in it, but all at once, the noise dropped to a low rumble, and with a thud, became silence. My eyes grew wide.

"Shit," I mouthed silently. We had an air lock. Airlocks happen, but this one couldn't have happened at a worse moment. We were almost to the objective; so close that I could literally taste the landing, and now, my whole approach had to be aborted. At 940 feet in total darkness, the ship was falling without controls, making its way silently downward. I watched with desolate eyes as the objective scrolled upwards and out of sight in my view port. This was not good. We were at 980 and falling so, in the tower, I started priming the pump and willing myself to think clearly because the success of this mission depended on me staying calm and somehow clearing out the blockage before we fell too far.

In any dangerous situation its always best to react on the basis of what you knew to be completely true, so I started ticking off facts in my mind: first, there were ballast tanks on either side of my craft, so if I wanted to slow down or go up, I had to rely on a hydraulic pump system that replaced the seawater in the tanks with air. The more air in the tanks, the slower we would go from the buoyancy, and the more seawater in them, the faster we would sink. Fortunately, I had managed to blow some pretty good air into the tanks and slow us down right before the system froze, so I had a respectable amount of time to fix the problem. Still, we were sinking, so I had to act fast. The block was being caused by a too-large bubble of pressurized air that the pumps had just sucked in from the cabin, clogging the tank lines like a painful, unfulfilled belch after a big swig of soda.

Ordinarily, I prime the pump just before take-off and again at about 600 feet. That's halfway to depth so it's a good marker for me to remember to clear them, but there was nothing ordinary about this dive. I'd been concentrating so hard on seeing the upcoming Haystacks at 600 feet that I couldn't pay attention to anything else, and I simply forgot. It was too dicey a moment for me to turn my eyes away. By the time we'd arrived at nine hundred feet and all was lucid again, I turned on the pump valves and trusted they'd be fine, which they usually are, but the system was greedy for air. It sucked down more than it could handle, the bubble was stuck, and now nothing was getting in or out of those tanks until I blew the lines clean. The only question was how.

We were at 1000 feet and falling faster. The emergency blow was an option, but not the best one. A few months before this dive, a maintenance team in the North Sea had done a test run on a similar sub and encountered an air lock like the one I was experiencing. They decided to engage the blow to bring her back up but when they turned on the valve, nothing happened. Apparently, the tech on the dive was a newbie and didn't know enough to be sure he'd opened the HP air bottles that provide the soft ballast air during his pre-dive checks. Even though the emergency tanks were loaded with the high pressure air they would desperately need to surface and survive, it was totally inaccessible. They were sinking with no way to stop the sub, period, and stark terror was usually an absolute fount of inspiration. The maintenance crew whipped up a very creative solution very quickly. They decided to open up the tanks as far as they could go and let the outside water pressure move through the lines full force, like a blasting fire hose, sinking the sub farther down at first, but blowing out the air lock and making it possible to empty the tanks of the ballast water. It worked, and they stopped the sub's descent at

1450 feet, a mere fifty feet short of everyone inside meeting their creator.

We weren't that desperate. The air bottles on my pre-dive check were fine, but I was a real stickler for not using emergency resources unless I absolutely had to. An emergency blow required using the air supply, and air was a resource far too precious to waste on a submarine. In a pinch, I'd do whatever I could. I'd use all the battery power I needed, and even take a chance on blowing seawater through the lines, but when all I had on board was a seven-day life support system, including air, you could bet I was going to want to hoard as much of it as I could. I had about 350 feet left to fall before we were in really deep shit, so I decided water was the better choice.

It worked for those guys, I thought. It oughta work for us.

I turned on the lights, and started priming the pump for all I was worth. The lines had to be ready to accept the outside pressure of 450 pounds per square inch, a power equal to a million pounds of weight pressing against the view port alone. The full force of the Caribbean Sea was about to shoot through the plumbing of my tiny submersible like a geyser and blow that damn air lock, and hopefully nothing else, right out of the sub.

I looked at the gauge and we were at 1150 feet. I pushed the knob in and out so quickly my hand was a blur, and with a whoosh, the pumps responded. I could hear the glorious sound of water running full blast through the lines and, though it was probably just my imagination, the air lock fart seemed to give the ship an infinitesimal extra thrust through the water as it broke free. The lines were clear, and I didn't have to waste so much as one breath of our invaluable air supply. Both my heartbeat and the sub's decent slowed considerably, and as I regained my composure, I started to casually head back up and east towards the mountain.

Penny asked, "Will we be landing soon?" Neither passenger was even remotely aware that we had almost taken PC1203 to her limits.

But nothing came easy in the deep. The minute I could look up again and survey the landscape, I realized there was nothing familiar outside my tower, again. During the whole ordeal, I hadn't paid attention to where we were falling, only that we were falling, and a quick flick of the lights on the wall revealed no identifiable markers. At least I was back in full control of the ship and moving at a crawl, so the disorientation I felt now was nowhere near as dangerous, or as nerve-racking, as it had been on the way down. At that depth and in that area, I felt comfortable enough to grope my way around in the shadows until I rediscovered the target. I just had to accept the fact that the search was going to take awhile and, after about an hour of looking to find a site that was only 150 feet away, we arrived again at Penny's Pinnacle. It was time to land the tuna.

"This is it then?" asked Penny in her unflappable Imperial accent. Her composed tone was betrayed by eyes that shone with excitement right through in the darkness. "Did you need us to watch the bait for you?"

I did. The tuna landing was the most critical part of this entire process and I usually had to encourage the crew to get involved. Plainly though, this crew was just a few IQ points ahead of the normal bunch of open-mouthed sightseers who fogged up my portholes. Penny and Tom's take-home pay depended on our putting the tuna down just right, so they were way ahead of me on the landing. During the entire descent, they had been forced to sit there, quiet and white knuckled, trusting that the oddball in the tower knew what he was doing as he dodged rocks and roamed around in the dark for an extra hour before finding the pinnacle. Now, it was their turn. They leaned into the window, and peered out eagerly trying to locate the lure below. I certainly needed the extra sight.

From my perch in the tower, it's almost impossible for me to see any bait trailing on the crash bar below. The best I can manage was a look over the passenger's shoulders and out the bubble, barely making out a grayish blob floating around outside the sub. I was sure that today's blob was the tuna, but for as clearly as I could see the damn thing, it might as well have been Esther Williams backstroking by. In their far superior vantage, Penny and Tom had a shark's eye view of precisely where the tuna was dangling on its line and, more importantly, where we should place it on the landing site. Monitoring my progress as the fish swayed in the current just above the ledge, they called directions out to me in an intense game of "warmer/colder" and I aligned the sub. Tom took the lead in this because he was the man with the true Vision for how the film should look.

"Back a little more towards the rock, I think, Gary," he said. Then he changed his mind "No, a bit forward I think."

He sounded like my mother when she cons me into rearranging her furniture. I wasn't about to argue with the guy, though.

Tom Fitz is an Emmy award winning cinematographer who has gotten shots so beautiful they could move Osama bin Laden to tears. I would gladly adjust the ship all night to suit any spatial minutia he required to work his magic.

"That's it!" he cried happily, and we all winced at the eager pitch of his voice. Everything was echoed in the metal walls of the sub. He cleared his throat and said in a lower tone, "I think we can put it down right here."

I obeyed and, ever so slowly, dropped the bait straight down. I listened for the signal from Tom that the tuna was touching the ledge and, when the fish lay flat, I stopped the sub and hovered ten feet above it, careful not to disturb its position. From that spot, I gingerly backed away, going no faster than a snail's pace, until the line between the tuna and the sub was fully extended. If I'd gone even one inch farther, I would have started to drag the fish across the ground and knocked it from its carefully chosen roost. We lucked out and it stayed put. Tom gave me the okay to put down and, in a little puff of silt, I set the sub in front of the tuna, 15 feet away on a tiny ledge that lay 1000 feet below the ocean's surface. It was a perfect landing, and it had only taken one and a half hours, six wide-open eyes, and three eager hearts to make it happen.

Now, we were deep in the mezopelagic zone. There was no more surreal setting in this world, or perhaps any other world, than what could be found in the deep sea at night. Salvador Dali in the middle of a fever dream could never have imagined such a place. With the sub's lights off, none of us were able to tell if our eyes were open or shut. All was darkness because frightened creatures had zoomed away from our noisy approach, but in no time, distant diamonds began sparkling in the surrounding water, swirling in the atmosphere like fireflies buzzing around a backyard barbeque on a hot Corpus Christi night. We went to red on our outside lights and trained the scarlet spotlight on the main attraction, the bleeding tuna. The fresh smelly carcass, as fascinating as a juicy steak under a hot red lamp to these bottom dwellers, immediately began to attract attention. Small crabs and brittle stars came first, scuttling cautiously from different directions to get a closer look at the unbelievable bounty that had miraculously fallen from their sky. Bioluminescent squid surged a little closer at the scent, lurching in a herky-jerky rush, filling the waters around our sub with starlight. Lantern Fish, whose flesh lights up in glowing dots came too, sending out their own special brand of Morse Code to their brethren; a blink to the right followed by a blink to the left, getting the word out that there was good eatin' to be had at the 1000 foot stack.

The "wows" started coming from the crew, and though it may sound odd, I found their astonishment touching. No matter how many advanced degrees a person might hold, or what scenes of misery or splendor might have callused them on the surface world, if you put any human being in the opulence of the deep sea, they were immediately transformed into a pie-eyed innocent. I needed a flashlight so I grabbed the one with a red bulb (so as not to effect my night vision) and shone it on the oxygen meter and the carbon dioxide Gauge to get a baseline. Carbon dioxide levels were a major concern during a long dive because Carbon Dioxide can become toxic to the sub's occupants very quickly if it wasn't properly monitored. In the event of a power failure, I even had a backup Drager that would manually check our CO_2 concentration and keep us safe. It was absolutely essential to stay on top of our air quality at all times because it is far too easy to fall asleep from Co2 poisoning and dream your way straight into the afterlife. There were worse ways to go, I suppose, but I wasn't exactly eager to die and miss anything on this mission. I radioed the surface officer on the UWT to let him know we had arrived in one piece.

"This is PC1203 Deep Explorer. We are on the pinnacle. Repeat. PC3 at one zero zero zero feet."

The answer came back. "Deep Explorer. We have your six, dude."

I couldn't resist taking one quick potshot. "Does everyone up there have all their clothes on now?"

There was a silence, followed by a rustling and murmuring before the one word response came back.

"Maybe," was all they said, and we laughed.

With the tuna in place and the sub acclimated, there was nothing left for us to do now but sit and wait, and wait. For five long hours we watched the Tuna while Tom and Penny recorded the action it incited in the vicinity. A little, plucky snapper was the first fish to brave the wide-open bait, going in for only a few sheepish pecks at first and then, once he had determined there was no danger in the act, becoming increasingly more aggressive in his attacks. He even took a run at the sub to show who was boss. Some of the crabs and the brittle stars that had already established a claim on the pink flesh hoisted a fragile, crusty appendage in a vain attempt to protect their portion, but the Snapper's lightning quick teeth forced them off in hurry. They stayed nearby though, rushing back onto the fish whenever there was an opening. A grouper with an oversized, slack jaw sailed into view and the Snapper, in his wisdom, turned tail and jetted into the darkness at his approach. Huge slithering conger eels braved the action around the tuna getting into interspecies battles for ownership.

It was all very engrossing drama, but it wasn't the Six-gill we were hoping for.

I'd been interested in learning more about underwater cinematography for some time and I noticed that Tom was being very selective in what he recorded.

"How do you know what to film and what to just let pass you by?" I asked.

"Well, it'd be great if my eyes were cameras because I'd like to get it all," he replied, setting the camera down and rolling his neck to work a few kinks out. "But you rely on instinct. Sometimes, when you're working on a shot that isn't all that interesting, something else will come into view that'll blow you away."

Penny started to tell a story about the time a The Blue Planet team was in Mexico, capturing a huge bait ball on film. A bait ball is just what it sounds like, hundreds of anchovies swirling around in a tremendous orb, like a giant, living bowling ball, rolling through the sea, and it makes quite an exciting movie all on its own. Through a stroke of good luck though, this particular ball had the cinematic benefit of all sorts of predators flying through it. There was Marlin racing in and having a bite, sea lions cruising on the outer edge, helping themselves to a fish of two, and plunging birds whose beaks were unable to handle the great quantity of their catch. It was a predatory free-for-all, when suddenly, from somewhere far below the rolling sphere, an enormous Sei Whale came shooting up into the scene. He unfastened his great set of Sei Whale jaws, the kind that look like they open halfway down the animal's body, and thundered past the camera, mouth agape, swallowing the bait ball whole.

A moment like this had never been recorded before, and at the very instant that the whale was gulping; shaking cameraman Doug Anderson heard the film run off the reel in his camera. He became quite a religious man that day, begging and bargaining with God, promising the Almighty all sorts of financial sacrifices and pious behavior if only he could have a completed shot of the Sei Whale. Somewhere wandering this world, there was a very poor and morally upright cinematographer, because this spectacular footage could be seen on the Open Ocean episode of The Blue Planet. The moment the whale disappeared from the frame was the moment the film ran out.

The tuna was lying alone now, host only to brittle stars and crab, so we all settled back into the quiet and became lost in our thoughts. Mine were about whales. I looked out into the sea-night and recalled the Humpback I had engaged in Maui, Hawaii. There was something so special about whales. They really did take your breath away. Their speed, their curious personality, and most especially their size, dwarf humans so completely that people could almost feel themselves shrinking in their skin as the whales approached. And yet, as immense as the largest humpback may be, the water that surrounded him was big enough to swallow a million goliaths just like him, offering them all room to roam in herds around the continents, and still managed to keep their secret world virtually hidden from man's view. I was overcome with a need to find out what was out there, and as I stared at four bioluminescent lights in the distance, I wondered if the creators of those lights were looking back at me.

I sat up and leaned forward. The four lights in the distance; something was very odd about them. They appeared to be about ten feet apart from each other, but they weren't independently floating about like four individual fish might be. They were moving together on a straight line, like a see saw, back and forth, four glowing portholes on a rocking ship. My heart flickered, and I poked my head down from the tower.

"Penny?" I asked calmly. "Could you come up here for a moment and take a look at this?"

"Sure," she said, turning around. She laid aside some notes and crawled into the tower. "What is it?" she asked. She was standing in the tower with her head next to mine so she could get a good view.

"See the four lights to starboard?" I asked, pointing.

She squinted in to the void. "Yes. What are they?"

I laughed. "That's what I'm asking you," I said, then tossed my head in their direction. "Watch the way they move. Do you see? I thought they might be four flashlight fish at first, but no way. They stay conjoined like that, all fixed onto one plane and parallel to the sub." I put my fingertips together in front of me and raised my elbows, rocking the plane of my arms for emphasis. "None of the lights ever moves out of line."

Penny watched the lights, brow down in concentration, as they rocked hypnotically for a long, long time.

"Well," she said finally sighing and relaxing her expression. "If that is a single animal, it looks to me like it's about forty feet long and interested in us." She slapped me on the shoulder and winked. "Let's hope it comes into camera range."

Penny crawled back to the crew seat and said nothing more, but I kept an eye on the glowing thing and turned the sub's lights on every so often to see if I could get a better look. Whenever I lit up the sub, the glow would slowly move out of sight only to re-emerge when the subs lights were off again. Every once in a while, Penny would ask if

the thing was still out there since neither she nor Tom could see it from the big fish-eye view port, and I would offer a report. Yes, it was nearby. No, it was drifting away. It was only visible from the tower and for a solid hour, I watched it intently. To this day, I have no explanation for the event, but I was fairly certain that I got to run into this individual again.

It was about ten thirty at night and dead quiet on the ocean floor except for the faint sound of a fishing boat passing by. The ship was probably 2000 feet off our port and a thousand feet above us. Still, we could hear it through our hull.

"Amazing how sound travels down here," Penny commented, and we nodded.

There was a constant cacophony of sounds in the deep, the

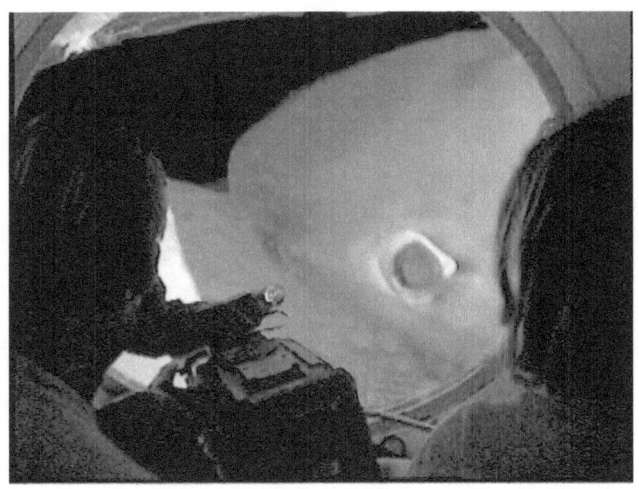

echoes of fishing boats, the sonar echo of our submersible
bouncing off the mountain , and that long, slow, scraping we
were hearing along the hull.

Penny sat bolt upright. "What was that?" she asked.

I had no idea. I searched the area around the sub, but could see
nothing. Everyone instinctively put their face right up to the
ports. Tom had his camera already trained and shooting, but all
seemed clear. Even the sound of the fishing boat passed away,
and the sea looked lifeless. The tuna fluttered on the current.

Like a clap of thunder, a tremendous thud rocked our boat,
stopping our hearts cold, and a huge white eye, as big as a
human head, suddenly filled the view port. It had a dull,
black pupil rolling around inside it, examining the contents
of the sub.

"Oh my God," was all I could manage to say, as the body of a giant Six-gill slowly emerged from around the back of the sub. First came the head, then a trunk that went on forever, and though we waited breathlessly for the tail, the shark just kept passing before our eyes.

"It's fantastic!" cried Penny.

"We need light!" said Tom, "but not too hot." He ordered all the subs lights on. "Tell me if it's too much." he asked Penny.

The shark circled above the bait, nose toward the rock and tail by the sub. She was too long for the compact, twenty-foot space, and her tail flicked us again.

Having rapidly measured the Six-gill in my mind's eye against the rocks the size of which I knew, "She's twenty five feet at least," I said, righting myself. "Maybe bigger. And right on time, you guys!" I was trembling with pure knock-down, balls-to-the-wall, excitement, but Penny's voice was as controlled as if was watching a fish in an aquarium.

"It smells something," she said.

"That was the noise." I said, as if we all hadn't figured that out by now. Tom was completely engrossed in getting his footage.

"Is this too hot?" he asked, still worried about the brilliance of the lights. Penny, looking at the monitor for the camera's exposure, said it was a little hot but there wasn't much we could do about it. We needed the shot. Then, in an appealing moment of authentic, unapologetic joy, Penny's voice fell to a barely audible whisper.

"Bloody Hell!" she breathed. "That is the biggest shark I've ever seen."

It was the biggest shark any human had ever seen, and it was right outside of my sub. She was literally breathtaking. I was thrilled beyond measure to be part of this experience and even better to be sharing it with Penny and Tom. At some point soon millions of unknown people across the globe would see the events of that night on TV. We were involved in a historic event.

The shark continued to circle trying to decide if grabbing at the tuna was the right thing to do or not. In spite of our best efforts, the brilliance from the subs 3000 watts of halogen lights was blinding the shark, and she just couldn't see the bait as well as we'd hoped she would. The monster would pass over the tuna, breathing in the scent and cloaking the rock behind her in shadow, then glide away out of sight. I kept watch over her comings and goings from the tower because Penny and Tom could only see her when she was in front of the sub. We could all hear the scraping of her body against our hull however, and my biggest fear was that she would attack our electrical cables. A shark's head contained a complex series of jelly-filled ducts, known as "ampullae of Lorenzini" that could detect electrical activity as slight as the tiniest muscular contraction of a passing fish. They used these ampoules for hunting prey, though some biologists believed that they're also good for detecting underwater magnetic fields for navigation purposes. I just prayed our big girl didn't mistake the sub's electricity for a live tuna and take a bite out of the cables or knock out our oxygen line. That would surely mean a long, slow, suffocating death for us all. If it happened though, it happened. There was absolutely nothing we could about it.

"She's coming around again!" I cried, and Tom raised his camera to get the footage of a lifetime. By now, the shark was convinced that the tuna was ripe for the picking, so she dove down, grabbed the 65 pound bait in her jaws and shook it like a piece of lunchmeat in her clenched jaws. Blood and silt flew everywhere, blinding us and rattling the sub.

"I can't see shit!" yelled Tom, but he kept on filming.

"Listen to the flesh ripping" yelled Penny, and the sound of snapping bones could be heard clearly through the hull.

Days later, in the editing room at the BBC, Penny watched the incredible footage, and knew in an instant they had their climactic scene for The Deep episode in the series. They congratulated each other on a job well done, and left the room to attend to other matters. About the time they returned to their desks though, a terrified shriek rang out through the offices of the BBC and it sounded as if it was coming from the very editing room they had just left. Penny, and her office mates rushed back in to see what was happening. There, in the darkened room, was the editor, pointing and laughing wickedly at a glowing monitor screen with a skinny, naked man struggling to frog-kick across it, trying to tie a very big, very dead-looking fish to a submarine's crash bar.

I'll never forget that dive as long as I live. Not only did I make a life-long friend in Penny Allen, I got to witness first-hand the indescribable power and beauty of the Six-gill. And I found a new passion in undersea cinematography, something, for which, I owe many thanks to the skill and artistry of Tom Fitz. I would dream about six gill sharks for countless nights afterwards, even though Mavis warned me that such dreams could be a sign of trouble.

"There are forces at work in the sea, Mister Gary," she would say. "Sometimes they're bad, sometimes they're good. But a dream, it always means somet'in." She shook her head with certainty. "It's okay though. Agwe will watch over you." Agwe was the Loa of the sea in Haitian voodoo. His eye was on all the plants and animals of the sea, as well as the ships that sailed on it, or in it. Mavis told me that it was Agwe who would decide my fate at the end of the day, but I wondered why she was so sure that Agwe was looking upon me favorably. "Well, you still here, aren't cha?" she said, chuckling, "and besides, I made a barque for you."

A barque was a tiny boat filled with Agwe's favorite foods, like caviar, coconut, and especially champagne. Agwe was a God with very expensive tastes. A person of faith would take his barque to the shore, pray to the Sea God, and put it out to sea. If it sank, Agwe had accepted the sacrifice and promised to look out for the man or beast in whose name the boat was offered, but if it came back, well, let's just say that Voodoo wasn't the first doctrine where the answer to a problem lies in getting a couple more bottles of champagne. Agwe was a giver of life, a lover of youth, and a protector of the innocent. I was grateful that Mavis' offer in my name had been accepted and, for a moment afterwards, I felt invincible.

It turned out Mavis was right; dreams did mean some thing. In this case the insight came to me in one of those 3 a.m. in the morning moments that make you sit bolt upright in bed and exclaim aloud. In my case the exclamation was the somewhat less than apparently revelationary "it all fits!" After that I dropped into the first dreamless sleep I had got since the Six-gill encounter at Penny's pinnacle.

The next day I couldn't wait to find Jason. I repeated my 3 a.m. statement to him "it all fits!"

Unsurprisingly he looked blankly back. My next words made him look at me decidedly oddly "I had a dream" I said.

Rather than calling the little men in white coats to take me away Jason asked in a very patient voice " . . . and ???"

Then I walked him through it. The day we got 'lost' nearing the haystacks and got hit by the unknown force at 1150 feet down when ascending. The day the 800 pounds in the drop tray got dislodged.

"That" I said to Jason "was the day I first met a Six-gill"

No other creature that could be found at that depth, I explained to him, could pack that much punch and move so fast we didn't see it. When considering the likely culprits before I had discounted the Six-gill as living too deep and being too small to be a real candidate. Now, though, thanks to Penny and Tom and my dreams, I knew a 25 foot Six-gill could, and did, visit the one thousand feet zone the sub had been in that day. It was patently obvious that the Six-gill had entered my life that day with Jason. It was equally patently obvious that the mystery of that deep sea adventure had been solved and my mission to capture "the monster" on film accomplished.

This extremely satisfactory outcome to one of my own Cayman rectangle stories only served, however,to whet my appetite to know more. I burned to see and understand more of the creatures of the deep. I yearned to again experience the seas spirit; that spirit that I encountered at the Kirk Pride; that spirit that took my friend to live with her. I knew my life would be defined, and determined, forever, by these forces. Agwe had spoken.